Praise for *A Call to Cultivate*

"In a time marked by uncertainty and anxiety, what does it mean to follow Jesus faithfully? Strachan points us to a hopeful path grounded in Scripture. His book *A Call to Cultivate* offers a clear, biblical, and practical guide to flourishing in everyday life—from our homes to our wider communities. I thoroughly enjoyed it, and I highly recommend it."

—**Sean McDowell, PhD,** Professor of Apologetics at Talbot School of Theology, bestselling author, and popular YouTuber

"We live in a world ransacked by anxiety and riddled with fear—how should followers of Jesus live in times of such turmoil and uncertainty? In this timely book, my friend Owen Strachan lays out compelling, practical, and thoroughly biblical principles that enable Christians not only to survive in a broken world, but to flourish—to truly *thrive*. As Owen keenly observes, 'God is calling us not to abandon our world, but to *cultivate* it.' Read this book and be both challenged and encouraged by the truth of God's Word contained within—truth that is as relevant today as when it was first penned."

—**Jonny Ardavanis,** Lead Pastor of Stonebridge Bible Church in Brentwood, Tennessee, and author of *Consider the Lilies: Finding Perfect Peace in the Character of God*

"*A Call to Cultivate* is not about political conquest or cultural retreat. It's about a humble, God-glorifying obedience that leads to health, hope, and lasting impact. In Strachan's typical lucid and even witty style, his biblical exposition is engaging, his theological precision is insightful, his cultural analysis is optimistic, and his practical application is relevant to everyday life. Rooted in the gospel and realistic about our times, he offers clarity, courage, and hope for Christians who want to flourish in a fallen world while maintaining their joy."

—**Dr. Jon Benzinger,** Lead Pastor of Redeemer Bible Church in Gilbert, Arizona, and President of Redeemer Seminary

"In a society filled with technological tension and digital dreariness, Owen Strachan invites us to do the unthinkable. To press pause on the busyness of life. To slow down. And to undertake tasks aimed at the development of beauty and enjoyment: connecting, building, and especially, gardening. He asks us to reimagine ourselves constructing lives that are centered not on the spectacular but on stability, not on consumption but on cultivation. This book is for agriculturalists and urbanites alike—for all who are trying to reclaim a sense of dignity and worth in a dizzying and angst-ridden society. But most important of all, Strachan reminds us there is only one way such a quest can be executed successfully. We must do all things to the glory of the divine Gardener."

—**Jeff Moore**, Assistant Professor of New Testament at Grace Bible Theological Seminary

"Much confusion abounds today as Christians wrestle with how to live in our post-Christian culture. Some want to hide; others want to fight. But Owen Strachan offers an insightful, biblical way forward in *A Call to Cultivate*. However, don't let the seeming simplicity of his exhortations distract you away from the richness and profundity of the call to build houses, plant gardens, create families, seek peace, seek God, etc. As we exist in this proverbial Babylon, Owen encourages us to cultivate deep purpose, productivity, and prosperity to the glory of God. This book is a mature and much-needed wake-up call for this generation."

—**Nate Pickowicz**, Pastor of Harvest Bible Church in Gilmanton Ironworks, New Hampshire, and author of *Overcoming the Darkness: Biblical Help for Spiritual Depression*

"In an age marked by rootlessness, expressive individualism, and the quiet collapse of moral order, Owen Strachan offers a bracingly sane summons to recover the creational logic of human flourishing. *A Call to Cultivate* diagnoses our cultural anxiety not merely as psychological distress but as a metaphysical problem: we have forgotten that we are creatures made for place, order, limits, and love. Drawing on Jeremiah's counsel to exiles, Strachan recovers a theology of rooted presence—building, planting, forming families, seeking the common good, and seeking God—as an antidote to liquid modernity. This is not escapism, culture war, or technocratic self-help. It is a call to reinhabit reality."

—**Andrew T. Walker**, Associate Professor of Christian Ethics and Public Theology at the Southern Baptist Theological Seminary

"Who doesn't relish a good journey? But as good as any journey might promise to be, it's only made better by a competent guide—by a veteran wayfarer who plans well, perfectly times the launch, carefully maps out the contours of the trek, providently selects the most glorious destination, and effectively leads every step of the way. Enter Owen Strachan. He not only possesses competence in spades, but he matches that competence with blazing passion and searing biblical wisdom. An epic journey awaits you as you make ready to traverse the breathtaking terrain of *A Call to Cultivate*, with Dr. Strachan as your trustworthy navigator. This excellent masterpiece is more than a page-turner—it's a disruptive agent that packs a punch powerful enough to jar you into personal revolution. Read it. Savor it. Live it out."

—**Emeal "E. Z." Zwayne**, President of Living Waters and author of *Fight Like a Man: A Bold, Biblical Battle Plan for Personal Purity*

"Owen Strachan's latest book turns grief into gardens. Strachan doesn't just analyze exilic anxiety; he teaches believers to attack anxiety in the joyful work of personal cultivation—building, planting, and seeking shalom in faith that the one who once planted a garden in Eden can transform your parched lands into promised lands."

—**Dr. Matt Shackelford**, Lead Pastor of Central Church in Collierville, Tennessee

A Call to Cultivate

A Call to Cultivate

Overcome Anxiety by Thriving Where God Plants You

Owen Strachan

REGNERY
FAITH

Regnery Faith books may be purchased in bulk at special discounts for sales promotion, corporate gifts, fund-raising, or educational purposes. Special editions can also be created to specifications. For details, contact the Special Sales Department, Regnery Faith, 307 Fifth Avenue, 4th Floor, New York, NY 10016 or info@skyhorsepublishing.com.

Regnery® and Regnery Faith® are imprints of Skyhorse Publishing, Inc.®, a Delaware corporation.

Visit our website at www.regnery.com.
Please follow our publisher Tony Lyons on Instagram @tonylyonsisuncertain.

10 9 8 7 6 5 4 3 2 1

Library of Congress Cataloging-in-Publication Data is available on file.

Cover design by David Ter-Avanesyan
Cover art by Ella Strachan

Print ISBN: 978-1-5107-8659-2
Ebook ISBN: 978-1-5107-8660-8

Printed in the United States of America

To Ryan Carr, a skillful cultivator and a faithful friend

Gardening is, fundamentally, an act of hope.

—Andrew Peterson

CONTENTS

Introduction

I heard a voice, that cried,
"Balder the Beautiful
Is dead, is dead!"
And through the misty air
Passed like the mournful cry
Of sunward sailing cranes.

Gripped by grief after the death of his mother, C. S. Lewis experienced a palpable effect when he read these elegant lines. Though Lewis would grapple with atheism throughout his youth, the story of Balder the Beautiful, written by Esaias Tegnér and translated by Henry Wadsworth Longfellow, transported the young man upward, to higher reality.

By a later recollection, beauty lifted Lewis up: "I knew nothing of Balder, but instantly I was uplifted into huge regions of northern sky, [and] I desired with almost sickening intensity something never to be described (except that it is cold, spacious, severe, pale, and remote."[1] Lewis felt a similar effect when he glimpsed an illustration by Arthur Rackham in the book *Siegfried & the Twilight of the Gods* by Richard Wagner. In that moment,

> Pure "Northernness" engulfed me: a vision of huge, clear spaces hanging above the Atlantic in the endless twilight of Northern summer, remoteness, severity . . . and almost at the same moment I knew that I had met this before, long, long ago. . . . And with that plunge back into my own past, there arose at once, almost like heartbreak, the memory of Joy itself, the knowledge that I had once had what I had now lacked for years, that I was returning at last from exile and desert lands to my own country, and the distance of the Twilight of the Gods and the distance of my own past Joy, both unattainable, flowed together in a single, unendurable sense of desire and loss.[2]

In these moments, C. S. Lewis experienced what he would later call *sehnsucht*, a longing for a lost place of great beauty and comfort. Though it took Lewis decades to cross the line of Christian faith, from his youth he knew that he was made for more than this world. He yearned to go to a place of "Northernness," a place of great highness, even as he hungered for abiding Joy, lasting gladness that evaded him in a hard childhood.

You could put it this way: Lewis longed for a place where heaven met earth and the soul met God.

We Were Made for a Garden

There is just such a place in both Scripture and history. From the earliest days of earth's existence, the Creator placed Adam in Eden. In creational terms, God made a garden for us—and made us for a garden. We were meant, in the design of God, to inhabit a paradise, surrounded by life, beauty, and abundance. Eden was our home, and as such, we are a race that was created for garden life, life that overflows into the whole earth.

This garden initially thrived in spectacular fashion. It contained no disease-bearing bugs, no warring species, no calamitous weather. Eden was the place where, at the start, everything good was present and everything bad was absent. This God-designed and God-tended garden not only included humanity but also had been specially crafted for humanity.

Everything about Eden gave blessing and prosperity and delight to Adam and Eve. A thousand trees budded with delicious fruit; the songbirds performed their impromptu concerts; the flowers radiated color. The beauty of the first garden reflected in powerful form the beauty of the Creator and his good plan for his people.

But Adam was not made to sit around and smell fresh air. Adam was made for a great purpose. He was called to work in Eden (see Genesis 2:15), to cultivate that place, and to steward it for the future. As musician and author Andrew Peterson has said, "Gardening is an embodiment of hope."[3] Adam's dominion-taking centered in the call to make Eden still more beautiful, and still more hospitable for humanity. This was not drudgery; when Adam worked unto God, to quote the movie *Chariots of Fire* (1981), he would feel God's pleasure.

Eden was not a bachelor pad. It was made to be populated. With the lovely Eve, adorned with feminine beauty, God called Adam to not only care for Eden, but to fill it with children (see Genesis 2:24–25), tiny image-bearers racing through garden pathways in the pleasure of playtime. The biblical God loves life, and so—to reiterate a key point—he made the garden for humanity, and humanity for the garden.

God himself created that garden so that mankind could experience the full measure of his generous gifting. In doing so, he gave Adam just a single prohibition: he could not eat from the tree of the Knowledge of Good and Evil (see Genesis 2:16–17). Sadly, Adam and Eve failed to keep this command. Though they could eat from dozens and dozens of trees in freedom, they chose to trust the devilish serpent, breaking God's law and summoning God's just judgment (see Genesis 3:1–19).

The Beginning of Garden Hunger

Despite their sin, God showed immense kindness to his people in three important ways. First, he promised the coming of the Warrior-Savior who would crush the head of the Satanic serpent (see Genesis 3:15). Second, he clothed his people in animal skins, shedding substitutionary blood so that Adam and Eve would be covered (v. 21). Third, he blessed the woman with children, and Adam named her Eve as a recognition of God's gift of life through the woman's body (v. 20).

God showed from the earliest hours of the cursed earth that he is a God of great mercy. Yet sin had ruined the unspoiled peace of Eden. In righteous judgment, God sent Adam and Eve into exile, driving them out of Eden. This was no mere change of location. The loss of Eden left a deep scar on the soul of the human race. From this point forward, humanity would experience what I call "garden hunger."

Garden hunger is the desire we all have for what we lost in Eden. In the core of our being, we long as a young C. S. Lewis did for a place of *shalom*, a place where everything good is found and nothing evil can enter. In the simplest terms, this is the place where heaven meets earth. Deep in our soul and burrowed down in our psyche, we yearn to live in such a place.

Yet though the setting is beautiful beyond belief, its chief blessing is that it is the place where God meets man. It is the physical center of our spiritual life. It is where we have a loving relationship with God—unbroken spiritual communion of the richest kind. We were made for such fellowship. As bearers of God's image, we are relational beings even as God the Father, God the Son, and God the Spirit live in perfect harmony at all times.

We human creatures are hardwired for relationality. We crave intimacy, warmth, affection, and the deepest friendship. We want these blessings not merely because we are social, but because God is relational, and the relational God made us for himself. Augustine said it well: "You made us for yourself, and our hearts are restless, O God, until they find rest in you."[4] It is in the garden of God that we find such rest.

The Reign of Anxiety

Here is a hard fact about life in our time, however: such rest is hard to come by. This is because, from many angles and for numerous reasons, we are an anxious people. A major reason for our anxiety is the lack of stability so prevalent in our age. Indeed, the only constant today seems to be inconstancy. At the day-to-day level, here are some metrics that spell out the instability of our era:

- Approximately 40–50 percent of first marriages end in divorce.[5]
- The average American moves 11.7 times in their life.[6]
- The average American holds 12 jobs in their lifetime.[7]
- The average length of a pastor's tenure at a church is about 4 years.[8]
- Almost 40 percent of students do not complete a bachelor's degree within 8 years.[9]
- The median age of a first-time homeowner is now 40, an all-time high.[10]
- About 14 percent of American families reported food insecurity in recent days, an increase from 2024.[11]
- The median tenure for a CEO of Fortune 500 companies has decreased 20 percent from 6 years in 2013 to 4.8 years in 2022.[12]
- The average tenure of an NHL coach has shrunk to around 2 years, down from 3.25 years in 2012–13.[13]
- The average length of a Premier League soccer manager's tenure is 787 days—just a shade above 2 years.[14]
- The average person has 168 passwords for online accounts, representing an increase of nearly 70 percent in just over 3 years.[15]

These findings give us a clear picture of a society in constant transition. Change is the constant; flux is the norm. In such unsettled conditions, people feel deeply alone. Here is how one recent study from the American Psychological Association characterized life in America at present:

> Loneliness and emotional disconnection appear to have become a defining feature of life in America, as a majority of U.S. adults say societal division is a significant source of stress in their lives. . . . More than six in 10 U.S. adults reported feeling this way, while half or more adults said they felt isolated (54%), left out (50%) or lacking companionship (50%) often or some of the time.[16]

Part of what is remarkable about this study is that we supposedly live in the golden age of connectivity. What is called "social media" was hailed as the great bridge-builder of the human race. But shockingly, the reverse is coming true. More than six out of ten people feel alone. In huge numbers today, people feel isolated, disconnected, and troubled. They are human, made for relational connection and belonging, but they live in a profoundly *unhuman* way.

Ours is the age of the *post-relational life.* Many people have lots of digital "friends" but little connection to home, an extended family, a solid church, a steady vocation, people who love us and are here for us, and to a promising future. They are not in a stable place, whether experientially, spiritually, or physically; they are adrift. In a word, they are exiles, people without a place, without a home, without rest—anxious and unstable.

A Threat to Well-Being: Digital Immersion

As we noted above, our supposedly social age is not yielding a harvest of friendship. This is in part because we seem to find ourselves in the middle of a great experiment. This experiment is, in sum, to discover what happens to humanity when we embrace digital immersion—or, put simply, when we live on screens all the time.

There are different dimensions to this ominous experiment. At the technical level, we are witnessing the rise and spread of "transhumanism," the transformation of the consciousness and body of the human person into an enhanced technology-human hybrid. Transhumanism has not yet gone fully mainstream, but it has gained adherents in recent years.

At the more informal level, we have gone almost fully digital. A gathering storm of data shows us that widespread embrace of phones, "social media," and continual usage of technology has not led to a sunlit oasis of personal well-being. This is particularly true among the group that uses digital technology feverishly, the rising generation. This group, which has not known a life apart from omnipresent devices, consistently self-reports as deeply anxious, isolated, depressed, and even suicidal.

Social psychologist Jonathan Haidt has recently labeled this phenomenon "the collapse of adolescent mental health."[17] This is not a shy assessment; if true, it is a near-apocalyptic social problem. Haidt's case has serious backing, particularly the skyrocketing suicide rates among youth since 2010: a 91 percent increase among boys and a staggering 167 percent among girls.[18] When the kids are left to their devices, one thing is for sure: they are not okay.

Device-addiction is driven by numerous factors, all of which need major attention. These include the deterioration of the family, the loss of meaningful spiritual connection, the use of drugs, and more. But we cannot miss that, whatever the driving causes, our era of digital immersion is not only problematic for our youth; it's "poisonous," as Haidt concludes.[19]

The Ominous Advance of AI

Nor is our technological chaos clearing. If anything, it is intensifying. As I write this in early 2026, we contend with the relentless push of AI ("artificial intelligence") into seemingly all corners of our world. One example of this sweeping change is the prevalence of "chatbots." Chatbots allow people to converse with a non-person presented in approachable terms on their device. Chatbots thus blur the line between fiction and reality.

This is not all, however. Chatbots are taking people to dark places. In one example of this, numerous young men and women have committed suicide after following the "Devil Trend." Here is how one outlet described this phenomenon:

> Tracy had posted several TikTok videos in the days leading up to her death, including one captioned "my version of the devil trend." The trend involves users messaging friends or AI chatbots with the prompt: "The devil couldn't reach me, how?" The respondent then gives a brutally honest explanation of the user's perceived flaws or emotional struggles.[20]

In Tracy's case, the response she received pushed her over the edge. The young woman, a promising Division 1 soccer player, committed suicide not long afterward. The "Devil Trend" illustrates the real perils of our constant digital engagement, but also how hard it is to keep track of all that is transpiring digitally and online. Clearly, we have many reasons to engage technology with care, wisdom, and not a small amount of caution.

In offering this perspective, I am not an all-out tech skeptic—far from it, in fact. Technology has positively helped our day-to-day lives in many ways, and AI may have some good effects on our society in days ahead. However, we cannot miss that a no-holds-barred embrace of AI and constant digital engagement opens us up to many dangers—and the young men and young women around us are the most vulnerable to these perils.

A Culture in Chaos

It is not only our devices that have us feeling anxious, though. It is our society. Over the last ten to fifteen years, the West has suffered numerous ideological assaults on the foundations of our civilization. In 2015, for example, America redefined marriage, making it inclusive of homosexual "marriage." Around the same time, woke voices started trying to gaslight mainstream America into accepting that it was "systemically unjust." It was only the beginning of a long nightmare that has taken incredible resistance to push back.

Wokeness struck at the idea that America had moved past genuine racial evils of the past. According to voices like Ibram X. Kendi and Robin DiAngelo, no such gains had been made.[21] Instead, being a "white" person meant that you were a crucial part of systemic social injustice, for as a majority "racial" group, you had invisible power over minorities. You fomented this power at all times and in all interactions, leading to a culture that was actually far worse than in the era of Jim Crow laws.

At the same time that ordinary people were attacked as racist simply for the color of their skin, the country locked down. COVID-19 was a real virus that affected many people, some tragically. However, instead of quarantining the vulnerable, many national governments quarantined the healthy, a measure defying all logic and past practice. In 2020, numerous states created and enforced measures that left churches forbidden to meet for months in many places (even as pornography shops, weed stores, and casinos remained open).

As we noted above, a veritable gender revolution played out during the last decade, as well. This occurred first at the hands of secular feminism, as men were displaced from influence and—in many cases—leadership. The recent popularity of the concept of "toxic masculinity" among the left has wrought a crisis among young men, with many of them hearing that they are irredeemable and subsequently acting out of that misshaped belief.[22]

Hard on the heels of secular feminism followed the "transgender" revolution. For the first time in human history, Western civilization substantially embraced the idea that people can change their gender. Men can become women, and women become men. This ideology is supposedly progressive and enlightened. Humanity, we commonly hear today, is no stable entity, no God-made race. No, the human person is a *liquid self.*

A New Way to Be Human

In practical terms, this means that humans are evolved and evolving beings. Here are some of the core ideas related to this new vision of humanity:

- The biblical God is not the true God; there is no one true religion.
- Humanity is divinized; that is, we've evolved into a state of higher consciousness and do not need—as in past days—to follow God according to religion.
- We may have male or female anatomies, but our true identity is not dependent on our body.
- Our true identity is not created by God but defined and lived out by us.
- We deserve to be affirmed in our identity by others.
- We need not depend on God for anything but can "manifest" our own desired reality if we apply ourselves.

In this vision, we are always changing, never sure who we are, and isolated from the one true God. There is no deeper meaning in our bones, no structure in our lives, and no *telos* (purpose) in our existence. We have no soul; we are simply desires colliding, a tempestuous cauldron of instincts and urges, and we are urged to find an identity in all of that stormy mess.[23]

We should take particular note of just how much young men and women have been indoctrinated in such a worldview. The godless vision of the human person sketched above is the very same one that has been authoritatively proclaimed in many public schools, colleges, education centers, counseling programs, HR training programs, and more over the last ten to fifteen years in the West. Small wonder that many young people struggle to know who they are and how to move forward in life.

All this malformation has come at a significant cost. Here is one effect of leftist ideology: it has enabled the rise of troubling ideology from the far right. Antisemitism has gained traction again. Some young men have reacted to feminism by adopting angry patriarchal views, voicing their desire to "dominate" or "control" or "take dominion of" women. Kinism (sinfully privileging one's ethnicity in marriage and national identity) has become more popular. Relentless attacks on "white" people and "whiteness" have had the perverse effect of fomenting "white nationalism."

It is important to note that these positions are *reactionary* positions. Leftism has exerted a real and terrible effect on many people, and in response, it has made people susceptible to ideologies from the opposite end of the spectrum. In many cases, these people are angry and have been scalded by evil attacks. Though they may not know it, in this unstable state, they are manipulable—easy targets for those who would use grievance culture and identity politics to draft them into their causes.

This is not a good situation. It may sound strange after the progressive nightmare America has lived through, but these reactionary movements—sometimes called the "woke right," and with justification—could, if enough momentum accrues, warp our youth and destabilize our institutions. These matters deserve further consideration, but for now, it is enough to say this: it is not enough merely to be against bad ideas. We must also labor to help the rising generation embrace good ideas.

Comforting Truth from Ancient Times

We live in an anxious and chaotic era. But I have not come to curse this age, but to light a candle within it. If we will think once more about God and gardens, I believe that we will find the curative that we need for what ails us in these modern times. Not long ago, I heard a powerful articulation of this hope in London.

Near the end of the 2025 Alliance for Responsible Citizenship (ARC) conference, a poet named Joshua Luke Smith took the stage. To my great surprise, he said these stunning words:

> *I hear the voice of an ancient prophet speaking to a depleted people,*
> *Housed in the walls of exile and defeat.*
> *They are longing for a home they've only heard of,*
> *A city they're unsure of, a country where they hope to be,*
> *And it is to them this wild man comes with fire on his tongue.*

Smith was citing the book of Jeremiah.[24] But not just Jeremiah. As he went on, it was clear that he was citing a passage I loved but had never heard anyone quote in public: Jeremiah 29:4–7.

> *He descends with a word from the god that they have almost forgotten, and he says,*
> *Do you want a revolution? Do you want a revelation?*

Do you want to renew your vision and restate a broken nation?
Do you want to overthrow the systems that have polluted the minds of your children and your spirits?
Do you want to live in abundance and remember where you come from?
Do you want to do the will of God or at least undo the will of demons?
Do you want to see people prosper in every sphere and across every tier of meaning?
Do you want to live a life worth remembering? Do you want to leave a legacy?

After these piercing questions came the showstopper. Smith ended the point by quoting Jeremiah 29:5, where God calls his people to "plant gardens" in Babylon:

Well then, plant a garden.
Plant a garden in Babylon.
Bury your seeds in the soil that you've battled against for so long
Because this is the only world to which you will ever belong.

Years before, I read Jeremiah 29:5 in my devotions. When I did so, I was struck dumb by the beauty of God's call. His people lay in the ruins they had made, but God had not abandoned them. As he so often does in Scripture, God called his people to build in the ruins and to cultivate beauty in a place of despair.

Instead of embracing death in a place of defeat, the people of God were to nurture life as an act of hope. Smith's poem captured the essence of Jeremiah's passage. What he said from a London stage seemed to me to sum up so much of the Christian's approach to life in a sin-cursed world. We are not called to despair nor passivity. We are called to acts of faith, however small.

The Theological Vision of Humanity

In the charge to "plant gardens," in fact, I believe we learn the biblical secret to overcoming the anxiety, instability, and evil of our world. Through ancient sources, God is calling us not to abandon our world, but to *cultivate* it. We may only do so in a God-honoring way, though, when we actually know God. Knowing God is, as we shall see, not a part of the equation; knowing God is the whole shooting match.

The solution to everything that ails us is found here: *God*. God is the one we need. In returning to God, we will find the happiness and comfort we all seek. But we do not only ask God for blessings. We go all the way back and scrub away all remnants of our own wisdom. In this light, we do not seek to define our own identity, as many modern people do; rather, we align our self-understanding with God's truth.

John Calvin said it well: "no one ever attains clear knowledge of self unless he has first gazed upon the face of God, and then turns back to look upon himself."[25] We must know God to know ourselves. This is an exciting new discovery that people have been making for millennia. True freedom is not defining yourself and living however you want to live. True freedom is embracing God's worldview and living under God's glad rule as a God-made people with God-given identity.

Scripture teaches us this enchanted vision of humanity from its earliest pages in Genesis 1–2. Here is some of what we learn there:

- God is real.
- God made humanity in his image.
- As an image-bearer, every person has God-given dignity, worth, and purpose.
- God made half the human race men and half the human race women.
- Manhood and womanhood are not choices we make, but sexes we inhabit.
- Our identity is not created by us; it is created by God and lived out by us.
- We are not made to be affirmed by others, but to glorify God in loving obedience.

Unlike "liquid self" ideology, in biblical terms, we do not *create* our own identity as human people. Instead, we *receive* who we are from God. We are image-bearers; we are men or women; we have God-given dignity and purpose (see Genesis 1:26–28). These essential truths free us from trying to be a kind of tiny divine being and free us to be the God-made creature that we are. We are not made to be masters of our own fate; we are made to live for God's glory as humble servants.

No one has captured this truth better in language than Jonathan Edwards, who once wrote the following about man's God-centered creational design:

> It appears that all that is ever spoken of in Scripture as an ultimate end for God's works is included in that one phrase, *the glory of God.* In the creature's knowing, esteeming, loving, rejoicing in, and praising God, the glory of God is both exhibited and acknowledged; his fullness is received and returned. Here is both the *emanation* and *remanation.* The refulgence shines upon and into the creature, and is reflected back to the luminary. The beams of glory come from God and are something of God, and are refunded back again to the original, so that the whole is of God, and in God, and to God; God is the beginning, and middle, and end in this affair.[26]

Edwards means this: we are made not to create our own vainglorious rays, but to remanate—or reflect—the glory of God in all aspects of our lives. This is what we were made for; this is why the human race exists. We are not masters of our own fate; we are creatures made to exhibit and acknowledge the greatness of the Most High God.

The Call to Cultivate

But such material begs a question: What exactly does it look like to "remanate" the glory of God in everyday life? The text that Joshua Luke Smith cited in London, Jeremiah 29:4–7, clarifies this calling. Even as Jeremiah rebuked Judah's immorality, he unfolds a breathtaking vision of a life lived for God in a fallen place:

> Thus says the LORD of hosts, the God of Israel, to all the exiles whom I have sent into exile from Jerusalem to Babylon: Build houses and live in them; plant gardens and eat their produce. Take wives and have sons and daughters; take wives for your sons, and give your daughters in marriage, that they may bear sons and daughters; multiply there, and do not decrease. But seek the welfare of the city where I have sent you into exile, and pray to the LORD on its behalf, for in its welfare you will find your welfare. (Jeremiah 29:4–7)

This is, quite frankly, a shocking passage. For those familiar with stereotypes about the Book of Jeremiah, this biblical section is not commonly thought of as steeped in encouragement. In fact, the term "jeremiad" long ago entered into popular discourse to describe a sermon decrying social and ecclesial ills, a phrase deriving from Jeremiah's numerous scorching denunciations of sin throughout his prophetic ministry.

But Jeremiah's words here are anything but gloomy. What Jeremiah describes is a ruggedly God-centered existence. Take note that this is not a head-in-the-clouds kind of life; it is resolutely *earthly*. Life abounds in this charge from God; vibrancy and prosperity dominate the scene. In the simplest terms, there is work to do, and lots of it.

All of this God-centered activity is deeply meaningful. The context described here hums with productive and creative activity, as houses are built, gardens are planted, food is eaten, families are formed, children are born, the city is blessed, and overall, the people draw near to their God in gladness. Abundance is everywhere at hand, the blessing of God is everywhere felt, and the broader city of Babylon is engaged, influenced, and helped.

The Plan for Prosperity

Here is the wonderful reality: this ancient picture need not be a distant relic. We can live out a form of this vision today. We are not under Old Covenant law, nor are we exiles living in Judah in the sixth century BC. However, we can glean much wisdom and practical application from Jeremiah 29, particularly as we examine how its priorities come to fruition in the New Covenant era.

Anxiety can be overcome. Flourishing can mark our lives. God can fill our days with goodness. In each of the following chapters, we will take a portion of Jeremiah 29 and consider first what it originally meant, and second what it means for us (refracted through fulfillment in Christ). Our focus is not simply to pick up a few tips and tricks, though; our focus is on a grand building project, the construction of a God-glorifying and joy-filled life amidst a fallen world.

Here, then, is where we are headed. In Chapter 1, we will study verses 1–4, seeing that God gave his people bright hope by continuing to communicate with them and direct them. God, we shall note, is doing the same today, in our own time of exilic wildness. In Chapter 2, we will consider the call to "build houses" from verse 5a. God, we will see, wants his people to invest in stability, a particularly important charge in our age of liquid modernity.

In Chapter 3, we will trace what a "plant gardens" mindset rooted in verse 5b can look like for us. This chapter, in fact, forms the driving concern of the entire book. Instead of consuming the world around us, we can cultivate our souls, our environments, our vocations, our churches, and our communities. In Chapter 4, we will hear God's call to "takes wives" and build families from verse 6. We seek to "multiply" even in the hardest places of our fallen world, knowing that the family is a living garden planted by God.

In Chapter 5, we will devote attention to verse 7, studying what a "cultivation" mindset looks like for believers in fallen places. In Chapter 6, we will move to Jeremiah 29:10–14 and the goodness of relational communion, considering the matter of our own spiritual walk with God. In Chapter 7, we will move out of Jeremiah and trace how the mission of God developed after the exile to Babylon, moving into a broader discussion of the church's calling today.

Conclusion

Our age is an anxious one. We all feel this keenly. But even more than feeling overwhelmed and harried by the conditions of modern society, we have a deeper longing within us. Just as C. S. Lewis felt in his boyhood, we want to know God, and we want to be at rest. This is because we were made for a garden, for a paradise where God walks with man, where we enjoy the deepest possible communion with the divine.

Alas, we lost this relationship in Eden, and we are sinners just like Adam. Here is the amazing truth, though: God made a way back. Through the death of his Son, a death Jesus prepared for in the Garden of Gethsemane, we can know God savingly. We can have eternal life. But not just eternal life—eternal relationship with God. This relationship, though, does not begin when we die. For every Christian, it begins in the moment when we trust Christ and repent of our sins.

That moment is when we all become a gardener, a *cultivator* of all that God has given us. Just as God called the people of Judah into pagan Babylon, so he has called us into all the world as witnesses. In that confidence, we journey to home, knowing at all times that there is a God who makes deserts bloom. We may have lost the Garden of Eden, but as we shall see in the pages that follow, there is a greater garden yet to come.

CHAPTER 1

Exilic Anxiety

The Voice of Fear and the Voice of God

Thus says the LORD *of hosts, the God of Israel,*
to all the exiles whom I have sent into exile from
Jerusalem to Babylon . . .
—Jeremiah 29:4

I cannot say that I ever expected to enjoy a butterfly garden. For much of my life, in fact, I was rather indifferent to gardens in general. As a child in coastal Maine, my family kept a small garden, but I did not invest much energy in it, save to pluck my wayward baseball out of it. Gardens were everywhere in Maine, and what is ubiquitous tends to be taken for granted by callow youth.

In time to come, though, I developed an unexpected interest in gardens. In part, this came from moving away from Maine and moving into neighborhoods that were dense with homes with little space for the cultivation of gardens. Another influence came during a trip several years ago to Phoenix, when my family visited a butterfly garden. In a small enclosed place, thousands of butterflies played the world's largest game of tag, delighting my three children by landing on them, only to flit away a second later.[1]

When we returned to our home, I had a newfound interest in these unique settings. I am far from alone in taking note of calming beauty in an unsettled era. In an anxious age, it is no secret that we seek out places of solace, whether they are scenes of nature or beautiful indoor settings. Writing in the *Wall Street Journal*, Katie Roiphe recently explored the pull of calm "domestic interiors":

> These images are a bulwark against change at a time when things seem to be changing at an alarming rate. Dreamy photographs of baskets and exposed-wood beams and straw hats hanging on peg hooks quiet thoughts such as "Will my job be replaced by AI?" They may also be feeding a deep, childhood notion of home we carry in our heads, something we read in "Little House on the Prairie" or "Little Women," an idealized vision of family happiness.[2]

Roiphe has spotted a trend. As we saw in the Introduction, people all around us feel harried, overstimulated, and anxious. In response, they have turned to a surprising line of content on the Internet: quiet videos and images featuring everyday scenes. When life feels overwhelming, the ordinary rhythms of simple living seem downright restorative.

Anxiety Then and Now: The Exile to Babylon

In considering how anxiety drives us to seek solace, I cannot help but think of a people who faced difficult conditions in their everyday life as we do. Some 2,500 years ago, the people of Judah entered the world's foremost pagan city in 597 BC under bondage. The glory days of Judah were long gone, when David and Solomon built Jerusalem into a resplendent capital and the nation flourished under the kindness of God.

As they entered Babylon, I can only imagine that the exiles longed for peace, comfort, and the beauty of their lost home. They had endured an arduous four-month journey stretching 900 miles from Jerusalem to Babylon. They were the first, but not the last; the people of Judah came to Babylon in three distinct waves of deportation occasioned by the just judgment of God.

Babylon, a city in modern-day Iraq, was not a scrubby little exurb. This was the city of cities in the age of Nebuchadnezzar (who reigned from 605–562 BC).[3] Built on the back of agriculture, textiles, and weavers, Babylon kept up prosperous trade with many surrounding nations.[4] The fields that produced barley, bread, and beer were watered by levees and canals connected to the mighty Euphrates.

The city also brimmed with idolatry. According to one scholar, "Babylon was a great religious centre, known as the Sacred City. At its heart were fourteen different sanctuaries, and another twenty-nine were attributed throughout the rest of the city. This was quite apart from the hundreds of streetside chapels and shrines."[5] Babylon was a religious powerhouse, albeit one steeped in false worship.

One breathtaking monument after another communicated the power of Babylon's gods: the massive Ishtar gate. The temple of Marduk, called Esagila. The steeped ziggurat of Etemenanki (quite possibly the tower of Babel itself). The whole city asserted, in the most forceful terms, pagan wealth, sovereignty, and power.[6]

Scholar B. T. Arnold describes the city's spirit: "Even before the city played an important historical role, Babylon came to symbolize the worst kind of idolatry, involving the dishonouring of the deity in pagan polytheism."[7]

Babylon prospered despite its wayward religion. For members of the tribe of Judah, Babylon would have represented a kind of mirror Jerusalem. It was a resplendent city that teemed with culture and achievement, but not for the glory of Israel's God.[8] Babylon's darkness led "Israelite authors to characterize Babylon as the place of religious hubris and degrading idolatry," a place where paganism flourished.[9]

The Background to the Exile

Why had the people landed in this fearsome place? To understand this situation, we need to retrace about five hundred years of history in a few brief paragraphs. As of 1020 BC, the twelve tribes of Israel were united under the reigns of Saul, David, and Solomon. This lasted nearly one hundred years from 1020 to 922 BC. In 922, the monarchy split due to the heavy-handed rule of Rehoboam, Solomon's son. It would never unite again.

Ten tribes coalesced into the northern kingdom of Israel, while Judah and Benjamin formed the southern kingdom of Judah. For the next two hundred years, these two kingdoms knew many ups and downs—but mostly many downs. One morally compromised king after another took power as foreign nations menaced Israel and Judah. In different places, God raised up a righteous figure to lead his people, but in general terms, the people chosen by God to represent his glory on the earth drifted far from him.

Spiritual idolatry brought political ruin as the Lord withdrew his protective power. In 721 BC, the northern kingdom was altogether overtaken by Assyria, leaving Judah alone. In this time, Judah lived between a rock and a hard place, as Assyria menaced Judah from the northeast while Egypt threatened Judah from the southwest.

The godly king Hezekiah fought against the spiritual darkness of the Assyrian and Canaanite religions, leading the people back to God for a time. But in 701, Sennacherib of Assyria nearly destroyed Judah. The southern kingdom survived only because of righteous intervention by Hezekiah and Isaiah.

When Manasseh took sole leadership in roughly 686 BC, the people began to suffer. They did not stop suffering for some 44 years (642 BC). Manasseh practiced wickedness in Judah for many years, reversing many of the holy reforms of his father, Hezekiah. Local shrines were rebuilt; Baal and Asherah were again worshiped in the temple (see 2 Kings 21); children were sacrificed to Molech. Manasseh ruled Judah for decades, firmly establishing godless religion in the kingdom once dedicated to the one true God.

After years of decline, God raised up another righteous king in Judah. In 628, Josiah took the throne and sought to honor God in all his nation. The next year, 627 BC, witnessed the debut of the prophet Jeremiah. Jeremiah, as we will see in further detail, exercised a counter-cultural ministry from the start as he called the people back to God—a lonely task.

The Influence of Josiah and Jeremiah

Tectonic political forces shifted again. Assyria, once so mighty, began to lose its control, and in 627, Babylon broke away from Assyria's dominance. Nabopolassar made the break final in 626 when he defeated the Assyrians in battle and became king. Babylon's power only grew for the next two decades. Yet despite this fact, God protected his people during the reign of Josiah. Josiah cut right to the heart of the problems in his country: he barred worship of pagan gods in the temple in 622.

In this same era, Jeremiah worked in tandem with Josiah. He preached righteousness in Judah, destroyed pagan altars, removed wicked priests (or executed them), and sent godly priests to Jerusalem.[10] However, as of 609 BC, when Josiah died in battle, the people had not heeded his words (see Jeremiah 25:1). The son of Josiah, Jehoiakim, became king, and did not live up to his father's standard.

At this time, the Babylonian king Nebuchadnezzar II assumed control of the entire Near East. Nebuchadnezzar would rule from 605 to 562 BC. For his part, restive Jehoiakim of Judah did not like being under Nebuchadnezzar's boot-heel. In 598, he rebelled against Babylon and was swiftly put down, dying as he was deported to Babylon in response to his unwise insurgency. Jeconiah took the throne and tried to hold out against Babylon, but the effort was, as noted above, wholly unsuccessful. He was exiled to Babylon in 597.

Zedekiah took office after Jeconiah, and it is this period of time that we focus on in these pages. In this era, Zedekiah waxed hot and cold in his subservient relationship to Babylon. Even as the Prophet Jeremiah called for the people of Judah to settle in for a long period of exile, rival prophets sounded a different message. They wickedly told the king and the people that Jeremiah was a doomsayer, and that their deliverance from Babylon would come swiftly. This marginalized Jeremiah, leading to severe treatment at the hands of his detractors.

The Challenge of the Exiles

The fate of Jeremiah mirrored that of Jerusalem. When Zedekiah unwisely rioted against Babylon in 587 BC, Nebuchadnezzar swiftly crushed his rebellion. It was the end of the southern kingdom, and from this point forward the story of the people of God would be one of survival. The once-united nation of Israel—the mighty people led by David and others—was no more.

In the era of the Old Covenant, the story of the nation had ended. There would be no major restoration. The people of God would not rise up as a reconstituted force and take back the Middle East for God. They were defeated; they were deported; they no doubt felt despair. Commentator Philip Graham Ryken sums up their plight: "The Babylonians had done terrible things to the Jews. They had destroyed their city, ransacked their temple, ruined their economy, removed their leaders, and enslaved their populace. Babylon had done its worst to Jerusalem."[11]

The people Jeremiah addressed were broken, bleeding, and brutalized. In human terms, they would not have heard Jeremiah's remarkable words like a pleasant homily on a bright Sunday morning. They would have heard these words as a confused and almost hopeless people. They had lost everything, and the city in which they now lived was foreign and even hostile to them in many ways.

They found themselves in a strange place. They did not want to live under a foreign ruler. They craved lasting rest in a peaceful home. But that is where the story of their spirituality had taken them. They had wandered and strayed from God. Now, instead of being in their own city, the city of David, they had the status of exiles—and nothing they could do could change this condition.

The Comfort of the Exiles

It was in this precise moment, however, that God spoke to his people. Though the people had brought judgment upon themselves, God reminded them of his ongoing control and care for them:

> These are the words of the letter that Jeremiah the prophet sent from Jerusalem to the surviving elders of the exiles, and to the priests, the prophets, and all the people, whom Nebuchadnezzar had taken into exile from Jerusalem to Babylon. This was after King Jeconiah and the queen mother, the eunuchs, the officials of Judah and Jerusalem, the craftsmen, and the metal workers had departed from Jerusalem. The letter was sent by the hand of Elasah the son of Shaphan and Gemariah the son of Hilkiah, whom Zedekiah king of Judah sent to Babylon to Nebuchadnezzar king of Babylon. It said: "Thus says the LORD of hosts, the God of Israel, to all the exiles whom I have sent into exile from Jerusalem to Babylon. . . ." (Jeremiah 29:1–4)

We cannot underplay how significant this is. God had not left the tribe of Judah on their own. Though the people had dishonored God over and over again, he had not abandoned them in a moody outburst. He was still with them, still speaking to them, and still ruling over the myriad details of their situation. God communicated in no uncertain terms that he was in charge of everything that was transpiring.

The exile had not caught the God of heaven and earth unawares. God was the one who occasioned it, for in first-person language, he spoke through Jeremiah to all those *whom I have sent into exile from Jerusalem to Babylon* (v. 4). The people of Judah dwelt in Babylon for one reason alone: because God sent them there.

How wonderful to consider, then, that God kept covenant with them. The exiles of Judah were cast out of Jerusalem, but they were not cast off from God. As Jeremiah 29:1–3 shows, God had presided over every facet of the catastrophic breakdown of the southern kingdom (and the northern one before that, and the united one before that).

When in these verses God named the different groups taken into exile—the elders, the priests, the prophets, and the people—he revealed that every last exile was known to him. He knew not only the whole body of exiles, but the chief officials. God knew King Jeconiah. He knew the "queen mother." He knew the eunuchs and officials. He knew the craftsmen. He knew the metal workers.

Through this passage, God revealed a wonderful truth: he knows everyone and everything. This is not raw knowledge alone, however. God's knowledge is intimately connected to his plan.

Walter C. Kaiser Jr. and Tiberius Rata capture this point nicely: Jeremiah 29:1–4 contains "clear assertions by Jeremiah that Yahweh is sovereign over the country in which they are now exiled." This meant that God's "plan for them and his ongoing purpose in the world are not suddenly abandoned or seriously modified."[12] God was ruling over this entire sorry situation, and he was directing the destiny of everyone—from the king to the priests to the skilled makers—for his glory. Nothing was falling outside of his control.

God made all this clear as polished silver. It was not just that every word, phrase, and idea came from God, though. It was that the very *delivery* of the letter owed to God's good plan, coming through Elasah and Gemariah, men appointed to their task by Zedekiah, as Jeremiah 29:3 says: "The letter was sent by the hand of Elasah the son of Shaphan and Gemariah the son of Hilkiah, whom Zedekiah king of Judah sent to Babylon to Nebuchadnezzar king of Babylon."

There were two kings listed here. But in reality, there were three kings active in the deportation. One king suffered defeat. One king claimed triumph. But in all this, the greater king directed all details, small and large, to the accomplishment of his perfect purpose. The situation might have looked chaotic to the people of God, but God's revelation communicated a different message: God was not far off. He was with them, and working all things for good.

I Put You Where You Are

God did not leave this to speculation. In verse 4, the Lord indicated that it was he who had carried out the plan behind the exiles' deportation. As we noted above, God addressed this letter "to all the exiles whom I have sent into exile from Jerusalem to Babylon." In this situation, God effectively said this to his people: *I put you where you are. You are not there by accident. This is my world, and I am carrying out a plan that is greater than anything you can comprehend or imagine.*

These were challenging words to hear, no doubt. Yet though the Book of Jeremiah has numerous intense passages, this one is fatherly in tone and hopeful in character. *You are exiles*, Yahweh effectively declares, *but you are my exiles.* The people of God had not drifted outside the margins of God's care. Instead, God had acted to stop their slide into sin. He had brought consequences for their long disobedience. He was now replanting them in Babylon, but he was doing so not to break them, but to rebuild them.

As Jeremiah 29:1–4 reminds us, the revelation of God always accomplishes several purposes at once. Firstly, the Word *confronted* the people. It convicted them of their sin. This is what the exiles would have pondered as they heard God frame their exile as under his complete control. They would not have made excuses for their behavior; though led by wicked kings, the nation as a whole had moved away from God. The Word, then, first confronted the people, leaving them without self-justifying defense.

But secondly, the Word *comforted* the people. As we have sketched, God's words communicate the deepest possible solace for a suffering, struggling group of stragglers. The past was bad, God made clear, but yet God persisted with his people. He was not leaving them. It no doubt felt that way as they walked Babylonian streets and ate Babylonian food. But it was not so. The God of Israel was there.

Five Truths for Exiles Today

This material might seem obscure at first glance. But as we have seen, it actually contains great grounds for encouragement. The God of Israel and Judah had not lost interest in his people. Though they had strayed and sinned, the one true God persisted in loving his people and seeking their good. He had judged their sin, but his judgment did not cut off his grace, mercy, and kindness.

This is poetically relevant for you and me. We need to know these truths about God, for as we have seen already, we face our own age of anxiety. Like the exiles, we too battle chaos, stress, and uncertainty that swirls around us. Further, as the New Testament shows, we who follow Jesus Christ are "strangers and exiles" (see 1 Peter 2:11).

We will develop this theme in later chapters, but for now, it is enough to note that we believers do not only *feel* like pilgrims on the earth, homeless and adrift. In a spiritual sense, we *are* pilgrims. We are not home. We have not secured our place of lasting rest. Knowing this connection, I believe that we may extract five applications from the Babylonian exile that apply to our own challenges.

First, We Live in a Wild World

Consider the political chaos we surveyed earlier in this chapter. Think of all that the exiles of Judah experienced as their kingdom lurched from righteousness to debauchery to righteousness again.

Foreign powers menaced them. Hostile nations intimidated them. Evil rulers arose among them. Godly leaders sought to rescue them. The entire experience totaled up to a great amount of chaos and wildness.

So it is for us. On any given day, we hear about wars and rumors of wars. We watch as geopolitical developments threaten entire countries, even regions. Breaking news informs us of tragic events. Social media features videos of terrible crimes and frightful encounters. Our flight gets canceled out of nowhere, with no explanation. A good friend disappears from our social network, leaving us confused and saddened. Health problems nag us, afflicting us, with no easy cure in sight.

Our world is a wild world. When we study the Babylonian exile of Jeremiah, we gain valuable perspective on just how much swirls around us that we cannot master. We are in an unpredictable realm. It is precisely for this reason that the illusion of control is sold to us from every angle. We constantly try to secure that which we cannot obtain. We grasp for something fixed and steady, but it slips through our fingers.

This is part of why God wants us to study the old days and the ancient paths. They are not at all disconnected from our experience. We gain ironic encouragement when we see what the people of God faced long before us. They walked into uncertainty. They dealt with seismic change. They had to endure tremendous hardship, some of it self-caused. Through it all, God stayed with them. God helped them persevere. God brought them through their fiery trials into the safety of his presence.

He will do the same for us.

Second, God's Revelation Makes Sense of Our Lives

The people of God could survive their exile because God kept communication lines open. He did not leave them without clarity or direction. Instead, he gave the exiles the gift of his revelation. His revelation framed their situation; his revelation interpreted their condition; his revelation revived their faith.

The speech of God was not just a directive from heaven to earth, a one-off transmission to be tossed into the wastebasket after it printed out. No, the speech of God was a top-to-bottom rendering of reality. It drew the people of Judah out of their stupor, out of their haze, and gave them a God-centered perspective on everything they faced. This did not take the sting out of their sojourn, but it did mean that they could live by God's blueprint, not theirs.

We are no different than the Judahites. We too need God's speech. We need a biblical worldview. We need the truth of our ongoing salvation on our mind every day. We need to consult the map between earth and heaven consistently, reminding ourselves that we travel the narrow way to glory. We need regular confrontation of our sin, which study of Scripture prompts through consideration of the poor character of humans and the perfect character of God. We need counsel in our lowness, comfort for our hard days, and calmness in our troubled state.

All this God's Word gives us. The revelation of God is a gift of grace. Receiving it does not immediately resolve all of our problems. But with revelation, we gain the wisdom and mental fortitude necessary to endure what comes our way. Is this not one reason why many people around us struggle with "mental health"? It is not that they are more fallen than us; it is that they journey through life without God's truth, God's love, God's wisdom, and God's direction.

The point, then, is this: we all need God's revelation desperately. Without it, the world simply will not make sense. We will struggle to hold everything together, and we will feel like things are slipping away from us. But with it, with the Word of God, we will have the light we need to navigate the path God lays out for us in our exilic journey. We will not be lost; we will make it all the way home.

Third, God Is the One Who Appoints Our Trials

This is what the Judahites heard. God did not flinch from telling his people that their exile owed to him. He made this explicit in his letter of Jeremiah 29 as he spoke to all the exiles "whom I sent into exile" (v. 4). They did not land in a strange place by accident; they landed there by appointment. God, in the simplest terms, put them there.

The destruction of the two kingdoms happened because of sin. The Babylonian exile, we know with certainty, resulted from centuries of disobedience. This reality necessitates care as we think about our own lives. Scripture does not teach that hardship comes upon us *only* because of our sin. Nor should we think of our suffering as an automatic payback for moral drift on our part.

It is evident that God does discipline us as we wander from him (see Hebrews 12:3–12). It is also true that trials strike us for other purposes, often so that we will demonstrate persevering faith in their midst. Further, we all live in a fallen world, and so pain and suffering stalk all of us. When we suffer as the exiles did, we can know that God has not simply *allowed* our trials. Hard as it can be for us to say, God has *appointed* our trials.

Fourth, God Uses Our Trials for Great Good

Much that we walk through will be mysterious to us in the moment. Sometimes we will have clarity about out circumstances; oftentimes we will not. Why do we face this challenge? What is the purpose of this grinding circumstance? When will God lift his hand of affliction? We all crave clarity on such matters, but it may take time for us to find it. In much prayer and communion with the Lord, we can focus our hearts not so much on the specific purpose behind our trial, but on the work that God is doing in us.

As a real-life example of this principle, I think of Joni Eareckson Tada. Once a top athlete as a vivacious seventeen-year-old, Tada was paralyzed after a diving accident. She battled deep discouragement and even suicidal thoughts as a young woman. Yet something shifted as God worked in her heart. Her perspective changed. Over time, she found that her trials actually drew her closer to her Savior, Jesus.

Here is how, later in life, she reflected on this paradoxical process:

> The process is difficult, but affliction isn't a killjoy; I don't think you could find a happier follower of Jesus than me. The more my paralysis helps me get disentangled from sin, the more joy bubbles up from within. I can't tell you how many nights I have lain in bed, unable to move, stiff with pain, and have whispered near tears,

> "Oh, Jesus, I'm so happy. So very happy in you!" God shares his joy on his terms only, and those terms call for us to suffer, in some measure, like his Son. I'll gladly take it.[13]

This is the language of faith spoken according to the grammar of trust. You can only write this way when you understand, by grace, that God uses all things for his glory and our growth (see Romans 8:28). This includes our victories, yes. But it also includes our trials. Our hardships. Our extended seasons of pain. Our paralysis. Our occasions of humbling, when the consequences of sin have rippled across our life.

The presence of trial does not signal the absence of love. Hard as it can be to say out loud, God uses our trials to shape our hearts. This truth refutes a saying I hear people say from time to time: "Don't worry—God will not give you more than you can handle." No doubt, such counsel is well-intentioned. Furthermore, God often is pleased to limit our suffering, cutting it off before it overwhelms us.

However, as Joni Eareckson Tada knows, some trials do not disappear within days. Some trials linger. Some difficulties vie for control of our mind and heart, reaching across all aspects of our lives. We could say it this way: sometimes, God is pleased, in his perfect wisdom, to give us a lot more than we think we can handle. Again, he does not only allow such an experience; he appoints it.

He does not do so without cause. Much as we will often struggle to comprehend the precise purpose of God in our ups and downs, we need not be confused about God's general intention. God uses the hardest events, the grinding problems, to awaken us to our need for him. C. S. Lewis memorably made this point: "Pain insists upon being attended to. God whispers to us in our pleasures, speaks in our conscience, but shouts in our pain: it is His megaphone to rouse a deaf world."[14]

It is worth noting briefly that Lewis knew of what he wrote. We saw in the Introduction how he yearned for joy when, as a boy, he found happiness elusive. His later life was not easy, either. Even after he turned to Christ, Lewis spent years in a difficult common-law marriage, then watched as his true love, Joy Davidman, succumbed to the ravages of cancer. Pain had shouted into C. S. Lewis's life—but so, even more, had the grace of God.

Many years before Lewis pondered the meaning of pain, the Babylonian exiles heard God shout to them. They may well have felt abandoned by God in that moment. The opposite was true, though. It was precisely in their time of exile that God was reaching out to them and drawing near to them. Such are the ways of God. He brings challenges into our lives with a clear Fatherly purpose (Hebrews 12:3–9).

God uses pain not as a whip to scourge us in rage. God uses pain to purify us, prune us, and mature us (see 1 Peter 1:7). He wants us to see that he is sufficient for all that we face, in contrast to the world and the self that are wholly *insufficient* to bear our burdens. Our pain, to echo both Eareckson Tada and Lewis, represents the call of God to come and be cared for by a loving God.

Fifth, Because God Sticks by Us, We Can Endure

This is what the Judahites needed to comprehend above all. As they entered Babylon by foot, they entered a season of testing by faith. They were literally in a hard place. But God was with them. As I noted above, God had not dropped them off for pagan summer camp only to leave them stranded. No, Yahweh would stand by his people for every millisecond of their time in a foreign land.

The same is true of us. We need these words from ancient days. We can learn much from this season of trial. The faith of God's people is given from above, and it is a rugged faith. It can endure a great deal. It is not made for quiet days and peaceful strolls alone; it is not a vacation faith that cannot function in the ordinary grind of daily existence. The faith God gives to his people is a faith that justifies, a faith that sanctifies, and a faith that endures.

Knowing this helps us avoid what I call the "Trial Minimization Instinct." By this I mean the compulsion many of us have to tell ourselves that our trials aren't really trials. If we just slap a smile on our face, all the unhappy things will magically disappear. So too when a church member asks us how we are doing, we present a flawless façade, acting as if everything is gravy.

We all must put our trials into right perspective, of course. They will all fade, and they pale in comparison to the weight of glory that awaits Christ's church. However, we should not be Christian Pretenders. We should instead be liberated by the gospel to be honest—in appropriate and balanced measure—about what ails us. Think, for example, of how Paul told the Corinthian church that at one point, his trials grew so intense that he despaired of life itself (2 Corinthians 1:8). There was no minimization instinct there, that is for sure.

Honesty is essential to thriving Christianity. This is especially true for exiles. Whether living in ancient days or right now, we exiles do not have the luxury of wishing away our condition. We are in a long-term sojourn. We reside far from our eventual dwelling-place. We do ourselves no favors by pretending that we inhabit a pain-free space. We do not.

We actually give God much more glory when we choose honesty, measured honesty, about what we face. We testify to ourselves, our believing friends, unbelievers, and the spiritual forces above that we are not the sum of all things, but God is. God is sufficient for everything we endure. This, and not a cheerful countenance we contrive to present to others, is our hope.

In all this, then, we see that the Christian faith is not a "get out of chaos" faith. The harder truth is this: the Christian faith will, at different points, deliver chaos to our doorstep. We do not practice a trial-proof Christianity, then; no such biblical faith exists. In both the sixth century BC and the twenty-first century, our faith is trial-ready. It is built for suffering. It is constructed for chaos. It will not fail in hard seasons; because it is fueled by God, it will purify, transform, and stretch us.

This is a truth that pushes us to the limits of our understanding. The hardest moments we face are often the complete opposite of what they seem to be. They do not show us that God has abandoned us; to the contrary, like the exiles in Babylon, they show us that God is very much with us. He is working out a plan much bigger than us. He is doing things in us that we cannot foresee and would not have requested. But all that he is doing is glorious and good.

Conclusion

It is not hard for us to understand why people all around us turn to calming places today. When you are struggling just to perform the basic duties of life, a visit to a butterfly garden, pictures of a cozy bookshop, and videos of a serene interior can calm harried nerves. Ultimately, though, we need something far stronger than chill vibes and beautiful images. We need the Lord.

Thankfully, just as the exiles did, we have him. As those united to Christ by justifying faith, we know that he will never leave us nor forsake us (see Hebrews 13:5). He knows the weakness of our frame; he knows how challenging it is for us to face the conditions before us. He is not annoyed by us; he is not trying to get rid of us; he is committed to us, patient with us, and at all times working for our good.

This truth does not make all our challenges vanish. No, it does something better and stronger: it equips us to experience trials and not quit. We cannot simply survive, though; with the assistance of divine grace, we can thrive here.

CHAPTER 2

Build Houses

The Joy of Deep Living

Build houses and live in them.
—Jeremiah 29:5a

For years of my life now, some portion of my leisure time has gone to a surprising place: home design shows. I did not ever imagine that I would have opinions on things like backsplash design, cathedral ceilings, and a neutral color palette versus a French country aesthetic. Over the years, I can confidently say that I've learned much more about these elements than I ever would have dared to dream.

This is not my go-to programming. Personally, I tend to relax—somewhat strangely—by queueing up a war movie. But war does not calm my loved ones; shows about home design do, and understandably so. As I've watched this content, I've had occasion to reflect on the theological wiring that drives us to seek it out. As those who have lost Eden, and who live at all times with *garden hunger*, we have an abiding desire to be home.

This is true of us as a race. We humans are wired for stability. Home, after all, is where the craziness pauses and peace flows. Home is a haven, a sanctuary, and a retreat. Home is where we can shut out the noise of the outside, be ourselves without apology, and enjoy the quiet rhythms of the good life: home-cooked food. Board games. Singing together. A great book to read. Unhurried conversation. Prayer.

God is not indifferent about these pleasures. In Jeremiah 29:5a, the focus of this chapter, God gave the exiles of Judah this charge: *Build houses and live in them*. Babylon, we recall, would have been just about the last place for the men and women of Judah to build their forever home. Yet this was where God instructed his people to build. In a chaotic world, God's call was this: choose stability.

This call, I believe, echoes in our own unstable age.

Building in Babylon, the World's Largest City

The people of Judah had not come to Babylon because they owned Airbnbs on the Euphrates River. The people of Judah came to Babylon under duress. They did not want to leave Jerusalem, and tried repeatedly to eject from their newfound settlement. No doubt they felt that God had done them a great injustice, and they wanted to live life on their terms, enjoying the same favor that God had graciously shown Judah for generations.

But here is an irony of the exile. In terms of their behavior, the people of Judah *did* want Babylon. By their own actions, they had dared God to judge them for generations. In the time leading up to the deportation, the people of God were far more Babylonian than Israelite, living not like believers but like pagans.

Babylon had long since entered Judah, corrupting its spirituality; now, Judah entered Babylon. As he does, God gave the people what they wanted: he sent them to the crown jewel of paganism. In its day, Babylon was the largest city in the world, spanning roughly four square miles. Aristotle famously said of its size that in one battle, the city "had been taken for three days before some part of the inhabitants became aware of the fact."[1]

Babylon was a spectacle in every sense. On the east part of the city, numerous quays (large docks) facilitated trade, bringing imports from across the region.[2] Its walls reportedly rivaled its gardens as one of the world's great achievements, for Nebuchadnezzar built them in a brilliant yellow and blue, making them both formidable and eye-catching.[3] Yet one structure loomed larger than them all.

The Tower of Babel

The architectural high point—literally and figuratively—of Babylon was the ziggurat Etemenanki. It is likely that Etemenanki was the famed tower of Babel. If correct, then God called the remnant of Judah to build a house for his glory in the shadow of one of history's most powerful monuments to human pride.

In biblical history, Etemenanki represented the zenith of man's self-idolatry (see Genesis 11:1–9). The ziggurat climbed seven levels into the sky, reaching a height of 300 feet (with a base 300 feet long and 300 feet wide). Several thousand years later in the twentieth century, this height would still rank the tower as one of the world's tallest buildings. Archaeologist Robert Koldewey, a pioneering authority on Babylon, summed up the architectural majesty of Etemenanki:

> The colossal mass of the tower, which the Jews of the Old Testament regarded as the essence of human presumption, amidst the proud palaces of the priests, the spacious treasuries, the innumerable lodgings for strangers—white walls, bronze doors, mighty fortification walls set round with lofty portals and a forest of 1000 towers—the whole must have conveyed an overwhelming sense of greatness, power, and wealth, such as could rarely have been found elsewhere in the great Babylonian kingdom.[4]

The Babylonians built Etemenanki with spiritual purpose. They believed it rested on the precise center of the universe, the site where the god Marduk had created all things.[5] The tower enabled humanity to have unparalleled access to higher reality. The top floors of Etemenanki functioned as bedrooms for the gods. The Babylonians believed in gods of water, light, and heaven, among others, and thought that the gods visited their city.

The Babylonians, then, were accomplished builders. The common houses of the city, however, were more ordinary. Ordinary homes were two or three stories high and made of mudbrick.[6] Numerous family members lived in the house, which took shape around a small central courtyard. Wealthier families had the luxury of gardens on site.[7] The Babylonians mixed practicality with aesthetics, as their dwelling blended both worship and functional living.

Supernatural Faith in Normal Circumstances

In this pagan city, the exiles received the call of God: "Build houses and live in them" (Jeremiah 29:5). Commentator Duane A. Garrett points out the strikingly normal cast of this charge:

> The Jews in Babylon were not to despair of the normal blessings of life, including children. They were instead to set about building their lives. Marrying and having children means laying down roots and establishing businesses to provide for those families. Building houses and planting gardens means accepting that this place is now your home; you don't live in a tent, and cannot quickly and easily depart (even if the Babylonians allowed that).[8]

These words capture the spirit of God's directive. Amidst numerous monuments to paganism, the people of God were not to take up arms. They were to do something far humbler and simpler: they were to settle in and build a stable life. This life was anchored in a solid but unspectacular house.

As the exiles built houses, so they would build a life in Babylon. They would rise from the chaos of the destruction of Israel and Judah and walk into the future with fresh faith. This was what God now asked of his people; so it would be for the people of God, in fact, from this point forward in history. No longer would the followers of Yahweh overtake lost nations. Now, they would enter them, settle in them, and build a stable existence in them.

Living in pagan places is no easy thing, both then and now. Yet here is the clear and challenging truth: God calls us to live out a supernatural faith in the normal circumstances of a fallen world. This is true of non-Christian places, secular settings, and pagan societies. Our primary calling is not to overthrow the king or leader who rules our territory. Our primary calling, as we see in 1 Timothy 2:1–4, is to pray for that ruler:

> First of all, then, I urge that supplications, prayers, intercessions, and thanksgivings be made for all people, for kings and all who are in high positions, that we may lead a peaceful and quiet life, godly and dignified in every way. This is good, and it is pleasing in the sight of God our Savior, who desires all people to be saved and to come to the knowledge of the truth.

What does prayer produce, according to this passage? If God blesses us, it leads to rulers stewarding their country well. This in turn enables the church, the people of God, to "lead a peaceful and quiet life." What Paul articulates here resonates deeply with God's charge in Jerusalem 29:4–7. The ordinary call of God on our lives is not revolution. In many times and seasons, the call of God to his people is this: to build in the ruins, and rise from the ashes.

God Loves the Steady Life

God is not a frenzied racer. God is a patient God, and he honors the steady life. He commends a stable existence. This was true in Babylon in the sixth century BC; it was true many years later, when the Apostle Paul wrote to Timothy; it is still true today, in the twenty-first century AD. And now, 2,500 years after God gave his house-building charge to the Babylonian exiles, his voice still speaks. According to God's Word, it is good for us—his people—to pursue stability.

The Christian life should not normally look like a kite bobbing and weaving in the wind, flailing without purpose or coherence. The Christian life should normally look like a stable, calm, purposeful undertaking. In this model, we build rhythms. We invest in long-term steadiness. We commit—at least as much as we can—to a local church. We settle in a community. We build habits, create structure, and embrace discipline.

But what I have just lined out may sound different than what some Christians have been taught. In years past, some believers heard a different vision of godliness from their spiritual leaders. They learned that faithfulness equals fickleness. Those who walk in step with the Spirit, they were told, experience continual unpredictability. Sudden bursts of inspiration lead to split-second decisions, unusual maneuvers, and little spiritual stability.

In such a context, zeal (of a kind) may dominate, at least until burnout occurs. Steadfastness will not rate highly, however. In biblical terms, that is a problem. Paul taught the Colossian church, for example, that the gospel makes us "stable and steadfast, not shifting from the hope of the gospel" (Colossians 1:23). To the Corinthians, a people surrounded by paganism, he said much the same: "Therefore, my beloved brothers, be steadfast, immovable, always abounding in the work of the Lord, knowing that in the Lord your labor is not in vain" (1 Corinthians 15:58).

The passages I have just quoted do not mean that we cannot buy a new home or move to a new location. They do show this:

contrary to what we might have heard or experienced, God loves steadiness. In fact, God wants us to pursue these qualities with spiritual discipline, to build habits based on deep commitments of the heart and mind that yield a stable and steady life. Spiritual stability, we could say, yields holistic stability.

Godly Stability in the Age of Liquid Modernity

This kind of principle goes against the spirit of our age. As we discussed in the Introduction of this book, we find ourselves in the age of "liquid modernity." In such an era, stability is hard to find. Conditions change on a continual basis. The new normal is inconstancy, and people live in a kind of social blizzard, as the following metrics—cited earlier—show:

- Approximately 40–50 percent of first marriages end in divorce.
- The average American moves 11.7 times in their life.
- The average American holds 12 jobs in their lifetime.
- Almost 40 percent of students do not complete a bachelor's degree within 8 years.
- The average person has 168 passwords for online accounts.

There are more statistics we could cite, but these data points alone paint a compelling picture. Clearly, our world is an unstable place today. Marriages burn out. The moving truck shows up regularly. Before we know it, we transition to a new job or drop out of school. As we saw earlier, these trends and others have created adverse conditions for many of us.

The point in this analysis is not that change is bad. In reality, some change is good and needed. Speaking at a personal level, I have lived in numerous states, and I am glad that I have. God puts us in different places and uses our travels and adventures for his glory and our growth. This rings true in my own experience; I have been shaped for good by the winding path that God has called me to walk.

However, as a person both living in modernity and influenced by it, I must also note the effects of much change. Writing after years of transition, I feel the effects of the multiple moves I have asked my family to make. From 2008 to 2024, we lived in numerous cities. We moved for my job (teaching theology, most of the time), and I am thankful for the ministry given us to do. But it is clear to me, from the wind-swept vista of middle age, that change comes with a cost.

Indeed, at this stage, I find myself—like many others who have experienced the "liquid" nature of the modern world—wanting the opposite of an ever-shifting existence. So it is for many of us, I sense, that after lots of transition and upheaval, we have made a new discovery that is an ancient one: the settled life is a happy one.

More than this, the settled life is a *biblical* life. God's Word makes it obvious, for God called his people to "build houses" and "lead a quiet life." We who are tempted to spiritualize change and de-spiritualize steadiness need to hear these words. Of course, God sometimes calls us to change things up, move to new places, and take on new challenges. All this is good. But God also commends a life of stability, and directs his people to put down roots.

How Do We Find Stability Today?

What does this look like, though? If you have not had much of a playbook for steadiness, how do you activate it? What steps do you take to start establishing such patterns? In what follows, I will suggest three overarching commitments that can put us on a new track. We can leave liquid modernity behind and embrace a life of God-centered stability.

First, We Must Recognize the Instability All Around Us—and in Us

The first step in overcoming instability is to deal with it. This means facing our own personal weaknesses. Sin, in the most basic reality, has left all of us disordered in different ways. We will overcome instability when we first own the fact that we need to grow—in our own unique ways—in steadiness, discipline, consistency, and calmness.

Some of us have level personalities. Others of us are more up and down. Some of us love rhythm and structure. Others of us prefer to function more improvisationally. Whatever the case, we can all likely find patterns of thought, feeling, and acting that reflect a lack of sturdiness. Our emotional life may need balancing out. We may fly high and dip low on a regular basis, lacking mental ballast.

Instability is everywhere. We find it in the appliances that break down three months after we buy them, the sports team that changes managers five games into the season, the whirling centrifuge of chaos that is social media at all times, the school events that are suddenly postponed, the flights that get canceled with nary an explanatory word. We cannot make all this go away. What we can do is identify it and begin planning against it.

Second, We Must Pursue Stability in the Spirit

Stability will not start with tips and tricks for self-improvement. Stability for us starts with the Holy Spirit. The Spirit is one of the three Trinitarian persons and specializes in dynamic personal empowerment in believers that yields long-term maturity and godliness. We can put it this way: if we are going to be stable people for God's glory, we need the Spirit.

We see how important the Spirit is in Galatians 5:16 and 19–24. In this passage, Paul ties godliness to the Spirit in an unbreakable way:

> But I say, walk by the Spirit, and you will not gratify the desires of the flesh. . . . Now the works of the flesh are evident: sexual immorality, impurity, sensuality, idolatry, sorcery, enmity, strife, jealousy, fits of anger, rivalries, dissensions, divisions, envy, drunkenness, orgies, and things like these. I warn you, as I warned you before, that those who do such things will not inherit the kingdom of God. But the fruit of the Spirit is love, joy, peace, patience, kindness, goodness, faithfulness, gentleness, self-control; against such things there is no law. And those who belong to Christ Jesus have crucified the flesh with its passions and desires.

This passage contains a great deal to apply. For our purposes, though, we zero in the key attribute of the Spirit-filled life:

self-control. Self-control is at base an ongoing exercise in stability. Instead of character that shoots off in every direction, godly character flows from a soul at rest. When Jesus saves us, Jesus rules us through the Spirit. Over a lifetime, the Spirit's reign in our soul and body produces greater and greater self-control, and that self-control produces a harvest of godly character in all dimensions.

Stability, then, starts with the Spirit. It does not start with ice-baths, stretching rituals, meditation exercises, morning wellness practices, Eastern mysticism, or clean eating. Stability starts with salvation, with resting from our works-driven endeavors to earn God's favor. Stability begins when we stop trying to save ourselves and trust wholly in the shed blood of Christ for our redemption.

From there, the Spirit fills us, grows us, and controls us, as our will and mind and body are activated to pursue godliness in every area. More and more, we rule our tongue; more and more, we discipline our bodily appetites; more and more, we take dominion of our thoughts; more and more, we regulate our emotions; more and more, we perform godly actions; more and more, worshiping God pervades our daily lives.

Stability will not yield one effect; stability will yield an army of effects. All of them, though, proceed from the work of God in us. Said more concisely, all of them start with the Spirit.

Third, We Must Take Practical Steps to Embrace Stability

Personal stability starts with theological truth, but it gets practical in a hurry. As the Spirit grows each of us in self-control, we will see all sorts of ways that we can grow in steadiness. Actions will present themselves as avenues for growth. I cannot lay out an exhaustive list here, but the following are some steps to consider as you seek to embrace stability.

Develop a spiritual walk. To grow in stability, it is essential to prioritize the health of your soul. Toward that end, I encourage you to read God's Word daily, pray daily, serve others, and generally enjoy your relationship with Christ every hour of the day. I will say more about this in Chapter 6, but for now, it is enough to observe that we will not find spiritual stability if we do not build in habits that anchor us in godliness.

Base your life around a solid local church. As you consider where you and your family (if married) would like to live, do not make the common mistake of choosing a place without regard to a church. Instead, choose a location that offers some feasible options for congregational worship. This is a huge part of embracing stability.

Your local church will have a much bigger effect on you than you might think. The preaching will shape you; the fellowship will encourage you; the opportunities to serve will mature you; joining in membership will keep you accountable. When you think about where to build a life, consider with great care what church can build into you. Think of sound local churches like Spiritual Resource Centers (with no set monthly fee!) and prayerfully consider finding one that will leave you far more mature than it found you.

Aim yourself toward a certain vocation. Many of us have held an array of jobs. That is no evil thing, obviously. We have much freedom in this regard, and thankfully so. However, in the age of liquid modernity, I believe that it is easy for many of us to hop from workplace to workplace, not knowing how this economic transience is keeping us from needed steadiness.

As I have learned in my own journey, the structure of your vocation plays a big role in the amount of stability you know. It is not that we should never make a job change; the point here is that, as much as we can, we should build a vocation. I will say more about this in the next chapter, for vocation is at the center of the cultivation mindset that Scripture so refreshingly offers us.

Choose steadiness in eating, sleeping, exercising, working, and resting. Even as we pursue spiritual stability, we should not ignore the body. Too often, we treat our soul with care but neglect our frame, our diet, and our sleep. We must remember that the body is a temple of God (see 1 Corinthians 6:19). Bodily exercise is not of ultimate value, but it is of some value (see 1 Corinthians 9:27).

Our body, indeed, is not separated from our soul. Our eating and drinking glorify God (see 1 Corinthians 10:31). This is true of our approach to sleep and rest as well. The rhythm of hard work followed by rest is written into both the hours of the day and the calendar of the week, a structure set up by God himself in creation. Sleep is both a necessity and a form of trust in God (see Psalm 4:8).

Of course, it is not that you are a bad Christian if you sleep poorly some nights. Nor does the New Testament give us a weekly fitness schedule. But the point before us is important: the more discipline we embrace, the healthier we will generally feel. The healthier we feel, the more we will flourish under God's loving hand. Discipline is not a death sentence; discipline is freedom. Knowing this, we do well to take stock of our lives and pursue stability of the body wherever we can.

Move toward owning a home. Godliness does not require that you own a house. You are not an Old Covenant follower of Yahweh exiled to Babylon, after all. However, we should hear wisdom in these ancient words and consider it. Our goal is not to be unstable and unsettled; our goal, as we have seen, is to embrace a "quiet life." The quiet life is anchored in stability, and stability comes from rootedness.

Perhaps we should consider God's words afresh today: "Build a house and live in it." We have much freedom here, but it may be that we find greater joy in choosing to build a life in a given place than in a "liquid modern" existence where we own nothing and settle nowhere. Rootedness, we recall, is not evil; rootedness is a gift.

Conclusion

As we have seen in these pages, stability is hard to come by today. Many may have almost given up on finding it. But whatever trials we have faced, we should not abandon the quest for a stable and structured life. It is not far from us, nor is it out of our price range. Stability is not found in your "forever home," lovely as it may be. Ultimately, stability is found only in Christ.

This spiritual stability creates holistic stability. This is true even in hard places. In ancient days, God put the exiles of Judah in a hard place, but he offered them a pathway to peace. He called them to the deep happiness of the quiet life, the contented heart, and the settled home. As an anxious people who live in an unsteady age, we need to hear these words afresh.

Our true home awaits us, and we are not in the New Jerusalem just yet. But godliness in our season of waiting does not mean rejecting beauty and choosing discomfort, as if we should all take up residence in an airport lounge. No, God calls us to something much better than this: he calls us to build a settled life, and enjoy it, savoring stability and embracing quietness.

CHAPTER 3

Plant Gardens

The Joy of Deep Cultivation

Plant gardens, and eat their produce.
—Jeremiah 29:5b

It was a stone quarry that became a sanctuary. But not just a personal sanctuary. Butchart Gardens of Victoria, British Columbia, rates as one of the most beautiful gardens in the entire world. Long after I left this enchanted place, I thought about Butchart Gardens and its miles of carefully crafted natural flourishing. One of the loveliest places on earth came from one of the most ordinary.

Before it started to flower in literal terms, the property was a stone quarry. Men wrestled rock out of the hills and shipped that rock all across Canada and the Pacific Northwest. Robert Butchart made a fortune doing so, and rightly so. His wife, Jennie, saw another prospect in the same property. She faced the unusual situation of residing in a stunning part of the world—the far West of Canada—while making her home in a jobsite.

As the quarry gave forth its rock and the stonecutters moved to newer zones on the Butchart homestead, Jennie Butchart decided around 1904 that she would try her hand at a garden where no flower bloomed nor tree blossomed. Her efforts bore tremendous fruit over time. For years stretching into decades, Jennie Butchart oversaw the development of a brand-new garden. Grass was installed; trees were purchased; more flowers than one can count were planted.[1]

This was not Mrs. Butchart's instinct alone, of course. Throughout North America, visionaries spearheaded a variety of beautification projects in the late nineteenth and early twentieth centuries. Along with other factors, this "back to nature" emphasis inspired over many decades the development of the National Parks (in America) and a broader gardening movement. After a century of industrial development, North Americans fell back in love with the very first residence of humanity: the garden.

We Were Made for Gardens

As we have seen in these pages, gardens matter greatly to Christians. Gardens, after all, are not simply physical places in Scripture. Quite the reverse is the case: throughout Scripture, gardens are places of profound interaction between God and man. Gardens are where heaven meets earth; gardens are where God first walked with man.

But this closeness did not last. Ejected from Eden, humanity became a race of strangers and sojourners. Yet as we discussed in the Introduction, humanity as a race has never lost our longing for Eden, nor will we ever lose it. We were made for Eden, for the pleasures of God in the paradise of creation. We are a garden-haunted people, and we all have garden hunger.

Here is some great news along those lines: our garden hunger will find resolution. In Scripture, gardens figure prominently in God's prophetic promises for our future, and Eden itself does not disappear from the biblical imagination. For example, Isaiah foretold the renewal of the earth and the forming of a new garden: "For the LORD comforts Zion; he comforts all her waste places and makes her wilderness like Eden, her desert like the garden of the LORD; joy and gladness will be found in her, thanksgiving and the voice of song" (Isaiah 51:3).

In similar terms, Ezekiel 36:35–36 uses garden language to speak of the effect of the New Covenant.

> And they will say, "This land that was desolate has become like the garden of Eden, and the waste and desolate and ruined cities are now fortified and inhabited." Then the nations that are left all around you shall know that I am the LORD; I have rebuilt the ruined places and replanted that which was desolate. I am the LORD; I have spoken, and I will do it.

As another witness along these lines, Amos 9:14 further reinforces the hope of Israel that will dawn in future days. Gardens factor heavily into the equation: "I will restore the fortunes of my people Israel, and they shall rebuild the ruined cities and inhabit them; they shall plant vineyards and drink their wine, and they shall make gardens and eat their fruit."

In all three of these passages, God uses the image of a revived garden to signify the future of his people. Gardens are where we once lived; a garden is where, one day, we will live again. But this is not all; as we shall see in our study of Jeremiah 29, God wanted his people to cultivate gardens not in the comfort of Jerusalem, but in the strangeness of Babylon.

Gardens in Babylon

This is what God says directly in Jeremiah 29:5b. After telling the Judahite exiles to build houses, Yahweh said this: "Plant gardens, and eat their produce." This was practical counsel, to be sure.[2] The exiles needed food, and they were not going to exit Babylon in the short-term. In God's wise plan, they had come to Babylon to stay for most (or all) of their days. They needed to develop food sources that would last for the long haul.

They would have had some pretty serious competition in the Babylonian Gardening Sweepstakes. One scholar conjectures that Babylonian gardens "consisted of rectangles of cultivated land set among irrigation ditches, and sheltered from both sun and wind by fruit trees, themselves overshadowed by a few palm trees."[3] The Babylonians took gardening very seriously, it appears.

The greatest plot in Babylon was purportedly the "Hanging Gardens," rated by the Greeks as one of the seven wonders of the world. There is a fair bit of scholarly disagreement over this spectacle. Various respected historians of the past like Herodotus and Josephus fired imaginations over the Hanging Gardens, celebrating their splendor, but more recent scholars have suggested that the gardens may not have existed at all, or that they were actually found in Nineveh.

No definitive conclusion exists in the architectural record. For my part, I incline toward the view that the Hanging Gardens did exist in Babylon.[4] If this is correct, and the Hanging Gardens did enthrall the citizens of Babylon from the palace of Nebuchadnezzar, then God's charge to "plant gardens" resounds all the more compellingly. In a city that celebrated arboreal beauty and took great pains to cultivate it, the people of God were called to be a garden-planting people themselves.

The Importance of Cultivation, Not Consumption

Unlike the Hanging Gardens, however, the exilic garden was not intended to take your breath away. The people of God were not called to compete with this spectacle. In their gardens, the exiles would possess simple beauty and a steady food source. But even more than this, I suspect that God wanted his people to have a tangible reminder of a garden lost—and the hope of a garden regained.

This hope would not spontaneously visit the people of God. It would revive in them as they got down on their knees, dug up the ground, and planted living things. Hope for the future would come through dirty hands and believing hearts. The exiles were far from Eden, but they had a mission from God of the simplest kind: like Adam, they needed to cultivate a living plot of land, coaxing life from the earth.

Cultivation is a word that bursts with biblical significance. It differs sharply from a word that we hear everywhere today: *consumption.* In a *consumption* mindset, we passively take in content the world feeds to us. This content is largely ephemeral, of no lasting value. It is the social equivalent of fast food—you watch it, it satiates you for a short spell, but it does not satisfy you. You want more and more of it; you want to be entertained, but there is no limit to this desire, nor do you find yourself reaching a satisfaction point.

In our era, a consumption mindset works closely with a device-driven culture. Our devices, we've heard, unerringly spark happiness, overcome our problems, and—this is my personal favorite—"simplify our lives."[5] As we use our devices on a constant basis, we think that *consumption* will make us happy. But this is a promise so errant that I believe it amounts to something approaching a false gospel.

Here is what this false gospel feeds us: if we binge-watch the new Netflix series, we'll avoid boredom. If we curate just the right image on Instagram, we'll achieve lasting personal fulfillment. If we sign up for Pornhub, we'll have sexual satisfaction, avoiding the difficulties of a human relationship. If we play video games for hours on end, we'll find the happiness we hunger after.

In these ways and many more, we get lured into a funnel. Our life becomes plastic. We live on devices. We crave entertainment all the time. We lose connection to people, to causes, and to God himself. We live an artificial life, building nothing, risking nothing, and in the end, gaining nothing.

A digitally saturated, device-driven life will not ultimately make you happy. It will not feed your mind. It certainly will not save your soul; it will actually help you lose it. But here is some good news: there is a better way forward than *consumption*. It is *cultivation*. In what follows, I list out three elements of a cultivation mindset, engaging relevant biblical passages as we go.

First, a Cultivation Mindset Necessitates Patient Skill

Gardens do not thrive when you step onto your back porch and throw seeds onto the dirt. Gardens ask for a *lot.* You need to mark out your garden plot. You need to prepare the soil, painstakingly removing rocks, tree roots, and scattered brush. You need to get the seeds, sow the seeds, and ensure that the seeds have indeed landed well. You need to address certain elements of the garden that need help. You have to protect the garden against critters and bugs that will spoil it.

Gardens are one thing to talk about and another thing to bring about. A garden isn't planted in an hour. It takes a lot of time and tilling. Above all, it takes patience—a lot of patience. This is a crucial element of a cultivation mindset: you play the long game, just like Judah in Babylon. This work repays careful thought and wisdom. But a whole lot of patience alone is insufficient for fulfillment. We need to marry patience with *skill.*

The Bible celebrates painstaking skill in no uncertain terms. One man who exemplified such an approach was Bezalel. Bezalel did not serve as a priest; he did not lead Israel in a military campaign; he did not join Paul on a missionary journey. Bezalel plied his trade as a craftsman, creating the Tabernacle (the forerunner to the Temple). Exodus 31:2–11 does not hold back in celebrating the tremendous skill of this godly man:

> See, I have called by name Bezalel the son of Uri, son of Hur, of the tribe of Judah, and I have filled him with the Spirit of God, with ability and intelligence, with knowledge and all craftsmanship, to devise artistic designs, to

> work in gold, silver, and bronze, in cutting stones for setting, and in carving wood, to work in every craft.

Bezalel represents a clear and striking picture of a God-centered cultivator. The Spirit of God "filled him" and empowered all his "craftsmanship." In God's kindness, Bezalel possessed "ability," "intelligence," and "knowledge." He had the ability "to devise artistic designs," showing us beyond a shadow of a doubt that God values artistry. He was deeply creative and fluent in metallurgy, able to steward numerous expensive metals. He could cut, he could carve, and he could pick most any "craft" and make a contribution.

The Spirit empowered Bezalel—this is clear. Blessing poured out of this man and his vocation. But note that Bezalel had acquired skill over many years. His years of graft enabled a vocation of craft. Bezalel and his workers, for example, fashioned "the mercy seat" of the holy place (v. 7). Their daily work no doubt felt ordinary, as our own labor usually does, but it produced extraordinary items that facilitated the worship of Israel's God.

Bezalel opens our eyes to the beauty of skilled vocational labor. Beyond him, the Scripture celebrates such enterprise in no uncertain terms. Francis Schaeffer draws our attention to the artistry of the temple built under Solomon's aesthetic eye:

> For one thing, the temple was to be filled with art work. "And he [Solomon] garnished [covered] the house with precious stones for beauty" (2 Chron. 3:6). Notice this carefully: The temple was covered with precious stones

> *for beauty*. There was no pragmatic reason for the precious stones. They had no utilitarian purpose. God simply wanted beauty in the temple. God is interested in beauty.[6]

This passage shows us what happens when a believer adopts a mindset of working *coram Deo*—"unto God." Specifically, *beauty* happens. Instead of merely functional spaces or products, the worker becomes an artist, one who creates lasting work of an excellent kind. Such investment is not unbiblical or wasteful. Citing 2 Chronicles 3:16–17, Schaeffer points out another feature of the Temple that shows that it was a blessedly beautiful place:

> Then in verses 16 and 17 we read, "And he made chains in the oracle, and put them on the tops of the pillars; and he made a hundred pomegranates, and put them on the chains. And he set up the pillars before the temple, one on the right hand, and the other on the left." Here are two free-standing columns. *They supported no architectural weight and had no utilitarian engineering significance*. They were there only because God said they should be there as a thing of beauty.[7]

Schaeffer is right: wherever there is a heart for God married to skilled craftsmanship, beauty will result. Such beautiful endeavors richly glorify God. In a fallen world beset by the ugliness of sin, the people of God have a profound opportunity in all sorts of vocations to do excellent work with the mentality of an artisan. This is not only true in the high art world, though; it can be true in all of life.[8]

Cultivation is less a discipline and more a mindset. There is not just one job that requires skill; skilled work can be done in a thousand different fields. When we comprehend this truth, we set ourselves up to experience much greater fulfillment and accomplishment in the tasks God has given us to do. Proverbs 22:29 promises future blessing to those who cultivate their craft: "Do you see a man skillful in his work? He will stand before kings; he will not stand before obscure men."

All this pushes against the grain of our culture. Scripture does not honor those who do the least they can to earn a paycheck. Scripture honors those who approach their vocation as if it is a lifelong exercise in growth. They seek to develop skill. They recognize that excellence offers an undeniable witness to the glory of God. They do not simply seek to get a job; they seek to cultivate their ability in a given field, dedicating all their endeavors to God.

Second, a Cultivation Mindset Necessitates Patience and Effort

What is a cultivation mindset? It is the pursuit of God's glory through excellent work produced by skilled persistence over the long haul. We have treated the "excellent work" part; we need to think about the "persistence" part. In Colossians 3:23, the Apostle Paul presents the Christian work ethic in a single sentence: "Whatever you do, work heartily, as for the Lord and not for men."

Sometimes we get frustrated as believers. We face unique situations that the Bible does not address, and we wish it did. But here is the truth about God's Word: it lights our path. It gives us our marching orders. It informs, for example, how we are supposed to approach everything before us God gives us to do: we should "work heartily."

Christians are not a half-hearted people. We do not do enough to get by. We give everything we have because we work for the Lord, not people. We persevere in well-doing. Matthew 25:14–30 features just such a mindset. In the Parable of the Talents, three servants are given talents (prized possessions, essentially, for market usage). The faithful servants invest their talents. The worker given five talents "went at once and traded with them, and he made five talents more" (v. 16).

This worker practiced *skilled persistence*. He brought real ability to his task, and that was crucial, but equally as important was his dogged determination. We need more of this attitude today. Yes, work-life balance matters. Yes, you should cultivate joyful rest in Christ. Yes, you should pursue wise discipline in eating, exercising, meditating, and more. But so too should we persevere in our endeavors, striving to do good work, seeing work as a gift, not a curse.

This is simply what Galatians 6:9 commends in plain speech: "And let us not grow weary of doing good," Paul writes, "for in due season we will reap, if we do not give up." The Christian's persistence derives from a desire to honor God, but also from the glad awareness that God loves to reward faithful believers. Nothing we do is anonymous; all of our faithful work is seen by God, and will be rewarded by God.

Third, a Cultivation Mindset Necessitates a Godward Focus

By this I mean that we work with God's glory on our minds at all times. Paul wrote this to the church in Colossae: "Whatever you do, work heartily, as for the Lord and not for men, knowing that from the Lord you will receive the inheritance as your reward. You are serving the Lord Christ" (Colossians 3:23–24).

We are to work "for the Lord," Paul says. What matters not is what we do, precisely; what matters is how we do it. This is because, in every moment of the believer's daily labor, we "are serving the Lord Christ." With these words, Paul electrifies the doctrine of vocation. Scripture does not teach us that only pastors or missionaries serve God; Scripture teaches that all Christians serve God.

We are servants who serve God at every hour of every day. This is not, we note, a popular way to talk in the twenty-first century. We tend to get very excited about *non-servants*. We cheer for athletes who make $750,000 a game. We go to the movies of actors who have a full-time hair stylist at their beck and call. We follow brand representatives who make thousands of dollars for sharing a single social media post.

These careers are not necessarily bad. But let us not miss who our culture fails, by and large, to celebrate: servants. In general terms, the more servant-minded your position is, the more obscure you will be. But it is not so in the kingdom of God. God sees every servant. He watches as we work hard in anonymity. He sees as we forgive and train and love our children. He misses nothing of the unrewarded work we do, the extra mile we go, the sacrifices we make for the good of others.

Our daily vocation is not just paycheck-earning, then. Our daily vocation is service—service to God and service to man. Long ago, Martin Luther made this fruitful connection when he addressed how a soldier serves God, against perspectives to the contrary: "So, because it is from God that a soldier receives his fitness to do battle, he may serve therewith, serving with his skill and craft whoever desires his services; and he may accept wages for his labor. For his too is a vocation which issues from the law of love."[9]

Luther's point was this: where we work for the glory of God and the good of man, we act as servants. Being a servant was not a lesser reality in Luther's mind, nor was it in the biblical mind. The point of daily labor is not to be known or be rich; the point is to glorify God, as 1 Corinthians 10:31 states: "So, whether you eat or drink, or whatever you do, do all to the glory of God."

Those who cultivate—those who plant gardens in all of their lives, everywhere they turn—do not see as the world sees. We keep an eye on the horizon at all times. We know, by the work of grace in our hearts, that God's glory is even now dawning in the cosmos. God is even now carrying out his work of redemption and transformation in his people. God is even now planting a garden in this world, a garden that depends on the faithful cultivation of humble servants like you and me.

Ways to Cultivate Your Life

How do we cultivate a life of cultivation, though? What practices can we adopt to switch out of a *consumption* mindset into a *cultivation* approach? In what follows, I will share several ideas to help you reframe your life as an ongoing exercise in God-glorifying cultivation.

Cultivate Your Soul

We will consider this need at much greater length in Chapter 6, but for now, it is enough to state this: we must care for our soul. Our soul is given us so that we can know God in the fullest and deepest way. In a way that is hard to capture in words, we have the capacity to know God in deep fellowship and intimate communion. By learning and savoring God's truth, we can draw near to God and know that he will draw near to us.

Should we give God all our being, in terms of devotion and worship? Yes, we should. But far more than performing a rightful duty, knowing God is our greatest joy, our highest privilege, and our richest delight. We could say it like this: there is no greater luxury on earth than the luxury of deep communion with the living God. We were not made for small things; we were made for soaring happiness and the deepest possible fellowship.

Cultivate Attention

We have heard the warning of Jonathan Haidt already in these pages. Digital saturation among young men and women has led to the "collapse" of mental health in the younger generation. At play here is our most precious commodity besides time: our attention. What we give our attention to dictates the shape our life will take, for good and for ill.

Many of us use technology a fair bit today. I can scarcely think of a person who doesn't. But I would argue that the wise Christian is someone who knows the dangers of digital saturation and device dependence and structures their life accordingly. In the simplest terms, we must not be ruled by technology; we must rule it.

This means, then, that we should limit our digital engagement. We do well to turn notifications off and put our phones in the other room for hours on end. In doing so, we resist the tyranny of the immediate and opt out of continual online engagement. In addition, we should intentionally embrace the world beyond our screens, seeing it (rightly) as more important than what is on the little block in our hand.

Many of us can see that it is good for us to slow our lives down and interact with the people before us. For no good reason, we can talk to a stranger. Wave at our neighbor. Buy lemonade from the child fronting a lemonade stand. Hold the door for someone entering the grocery store. Serve our church on a work day. These are all deeply human actions; embracing them will bring many of us back into the "real world," where life is meant to be lived, and where many of the quiet joys of life are found.

Cultivate Deep Thinking

I assert this without apology: the life of the mind is deeply enjoyable and manifestly rewarding. But thinking deeply is not a short-term venture. You can't microwave it. You've got to build such abilities. Here's a great place to start: reading books. Reading books isn't so much a part of deep thinking as it is the gateway and pipeline to deep thinking.

To do so, of course, one must *pay attention*, as we were discussing above. At the risk of giving overly direct advice, I would argue that reading is best done with the phone in the other room, silenced and turned off (bonus points if you muzzle it with one of those tiny little restraining vests they wear in police procedurals).

In the same way we gain muscle from weightlifting or increased balance from aerobic stretching, we think more deeply the more we prayerfully force ourselves to do so. As we think more deeply as believers, we gain the ability to talk with people, reason with them, and remain civil in doing so. Most significantly, we grasp more and more of God's greatness, and that increasing knowledge humbles us even as it thrills us.

Cultivate Bold Action

The "plant gardens" mandate was clear but wide open for application. In Babylon, God did not constrain his people to a twelve-step code by which they would cultivate their surroundings. God gave them structure but also great freedom in living within it. This is characteristic of God's dealings with his people all throughout the Bible.

As Christians, God wants us to live in liberation as we pursue holiness for his glory (see 1 Timothy 6:11). This entails something wonderful: we need not walk around with weight on our shoulders, fearful of getting the will of God wrong. Instead, we can move through life with the wind at our back, free to do what we want as God blesses and leads. Pastor and theologian John MacArthur helps us understand this point:

> If you're saved, Spirit-filled, sanctified, submissive, suffering, and thankful—you ready for this?—do whatever

> you want. Do whatever you want. Marry whoever you want. Go wherever you want. Work wherever you want. Choose whatever you want. You say, "Whoa. Are you sure?" Absolutely. Because if this is true of your life, guess who's controlling your wants. Do whatever you want.[10]

What MacArthur means is this: we should not live in anxious fear of getting God's will wrong. Instead, we should go deep in God's Word, build a spiritual walk, pursue conformity to Christ, and pray without ceasing (1 Thessalonians 5:17). As we do so, we are free to make good decisions (as best we can) for God's honor and fame.

This counsel is especially helpful for over-thinkers. At different points, many of us out there need a jolt of God-centered confidence to move forward. We fear making the wrong decision and messing our lives up. But MacArthur reminds us of a marvelous truth: the Christian life is not a life of constriction and severity. To the contrary, "For freedom Christ set us free," Paul said (Galatians 5:1). The Christian life is a life of liberation and joy, and we should act as if this is so.

Cultivate Joy

God is not a miserly Lord. God is a champion gift-giver. Because of this, Christians celebrate all of life (the moral parts, that is). We love spiritual things, but said more precisely, we see all things spiritually. I am reminded on this count of the musing of C. S. Lewis: "I believe in Christianity as I believe that the sun has risen: not only because I see it, but because by it I see everything else."[11]

This marvelous comment speaks not only to our belief in God, but our ongoing joy in God. Because God is real and good, the world God has made is full of good things, and we are liberated to enjoy them (see Psalm 16:11). This is what the "plant gardens" mandate reflects: it directs us to God-centered action in a joyful spirit, even as it urges us to get our hands dirty. Joy does not come passively, then; joy comes when we pursue it. It is not a trickle; it is a rushing river.

Joy is not found only in our quiet time or prayer meeting. Christian joy is all-of-life joy. When we read Scripture, when we listen to a worship song on the way to work, when we have a great conversation with a coworker that overcomes a supply-chain issue, when we come up with a new design for the guest bedroom, when we hit a new peak in our training session, when we watch our child play with other kids, when we pray together as a family—joy is in all of this, joy is driving all of this, and joy is the reward of all of this.

Cultivate a Vocation

In our daily endeavors, we Christians do not only perform tasks. We are not merely trying to earn a paycheck. As believers, we seek to find a fruitful field that fits our gift-set, and we view that work not as a mere duty but as a calling. For some of us, our daily labor thrills our heart and fits our inmost inclinations. For others, our daily labor is not enthralling or exhilarating; we do the job because it is what God has given us to do and because it provides for us.

It is this God-centered perspective that makes all the difference. When we approach work not as a mere money-making exercise but as a Spirit-driven endeavor in skilled stewardship and vocational flourishing, we find joy that previously eluded us. We get a bigger vision of what our life is about. We figure out ways that we can contribute to our family, our community, our society, and even our world.

The secret to unlocking joy in our daily labors is right before us in Scripture. It is a *cultivation* mindset. In it, you and I do not think of ourselves as merely passing the time or punching the clock. We see ourselves as planting gardens in Babylon. We do not labor under dark clouds; we work *coram Deo*, unto God, with the smile of God on our faces like the midday sun. Our work will always challenge us in different ways, but the Christian knows the joy of God as we seek God's glory in our daily endeavors.

Cultivate a Garden

When I think of what a blessing a single garden can be, I think of my maternal grandfather, Daniel Dustin. Years ago, before my radar-developing grandfather went to glory, he planted an incredible garden in his backyard in lovely Lincoln, Massachusetts.[12] Even today, almost twenty years after I last saw it, I can close my eyes and see row upon row of living things brought into existence by my grandfather's hard work.

As a young man, I was too excited by the Boston Celtics to pay much attention to Grandpa's garden. Yet he successfully grew numerous variations of fruit, his own roses, and much more besides. His patience with the land mirrored his patience with me as his grandson. Grandpa lovingly pointed me to Christ, encouraged my call to ministry, and sent me the Navigators magazine in college. In spiritual things as with physical land, Grandpa was a cultivator.

My grandfather reminds me of musician Andrew Peterson. Some years ago, Peterson moved into the countryside of Tennessee and found himself drawn to steward the earth. In his book *God of the Garden*, Peterson shares his metamorphosis. I'll quote him at length:

> [M]y friend Julie gave our family the gift of a thirty-year garden plan. She knew I loved English gardens, so she crafted a blueprint for me to follow until I'm an old man. It's taken years—hours and hours of work digging the footpaths and packing them with sand before covering it all with pea gravel, building the rock walls to enclose the front garden, constructing the arch, weeding the accursed Bermuda grass.[13]

Peterson avows this about his endeavors: "I'm no master gardener, not by a long shot, but it's hard to imagine life without it now. . . . After being indoors for hours at a time working on a story or a song, the sun on my face and the nearness of growing things rejuvenates me like nothing else."[14] He observes that the rhythm of gardening is itself an experience of resurrection, and his writing elegantly entwines the physical and the spiritual:

> The garden outside my window is dormant, not dead, because I know tulips and hyacinth, daffodil and crocus

> bulbs are already crowning out of the mulch, patiently practicing resurrection. There's a tangible energy in the brown, brittle ruins of last year's cottage garden, because I have seen that patch of earth renewed by spring, and spring has begun its inexorable advent. I know it's coming, and my body yearns for it.[15]

If you find these words from Peterson inspiring (as I do), then here is some friendly encouragement. If you have time and interest, you could plant a garden. Perhaps, in and amongst the trials of coaxing living things from the ground, you too will "practice resurrection." If so, that will be no waste of time, but a little picture of what God is doing in us.

The Work of God Plays Out in Gardens

Whether we foster a plot of land or not, we should "plant gardens" in all of our lives. This means, at base, that we reject the consumption mindset so prevalent today and embrace a cultivation mindset. As we do so, we should also remember that gardens play a bigger role in our story than we might initially think.

We have seen this already in Eden, the place where our race both began and fell from God. But Eden is not the only garden that plays into the grand story of redemption. Like the first Adam, Scripture associates Jesus, the Second Adam, with gardens. In John 18:1, Jesus enters a garden—Gethsemane—to pray to the Father before his crucifixion. In John 19:41, we learn that "in the place where he was crucified there was a garden, and in the garden a new tomb in which no one had yet been laid."

Gardens feature prominently in the work of Christ, both as he heads toward the cross and as his broken, lifeless body is carried away from it to his resting place. To put the point more directly, Jesus prepared for death in a garden, and Jesus rested in death in a garden. Jesus also rose to life in a garden.

It is worth taking a little space to think about this last reality and what it signifies. After he died on the cross, Jesus was buried in the tomb of Joseph of Arimathea (see John 20). There, Mary Magdalene came to visit his body. She was distraught. It is no wonder why, for Mary had found in Jesus a good man, a strong man, a teacher, and a redeemer. Luke 8:1–2 gives us a quick window into her difficult past:

> Soon afterward he went on through cities and villages, proclaiming and bringing the good news of the kingdom of God. And the twelve were with him, and also some women who had been healed of evil spirits and infirmities: Mary, called Magdalene, from whom seven demons had gone out. . . .

In her earlier life, Mary Magdalene had not one demon tormenting her, but seven. But all that changed when Mary met Jesus. She had found in him her healer. Her teacher. A man who looked on her with eyes of love and called her out of the darkness into the light. Mary came to Jesus full of pain and sin, and found in Jesus peace and salvation.

Mary did not visit Jesus's garden tomb in a triumphal spirit, however. Just as nobody cheered at the cross, Mary did not exult in the garden. Jesus had clearly told his disciples that he would rise from death, but like us, they struggled to grasp the promises of God and apply them in fullness of faith. So it was that Mary drew near to the cold grave of her Lord in the early morning hours. Alone. Distraught. Troubled. And yet: there.

Mary Meets the Gardener

She came while it was "still dark" (John 20:1). The color of the sky mirrored the condition of the heart of Jesus's followers. Their prospects were as bleak as bleak could be. The Jewish nation was unled. The Romans were undefeated. The personal problems of the disciples remained, uncured and seemingly forgotten. Now, perhaps worst of all, they were alone. Their leader had been caught out in a vicious scheme, betrayed by Judas, and killed seemingly against his will.

What followed next came fast and furious. Confusion dominated the next few minutes and hours. Entering the garden, Mary found the stone rolled away and ran to Peter and John, supposing that Jesus's body had been taken away (v. 2). Peter and John then raced over to the grave, with John outrunning Peter (v. 4). The men discovered the "linen cloths" lying where they were left (v. 6), while the face cloth was "folded up" and tucked neatly at the side (v. 7).

The disciples then went home (v. 10). For her part, Mary Magdalene stayed near where the body of Jesus had lain (v. 11). She "stood weeping" over the empty tomb (v. 11) initially, but then things changed when she looked into the tomb. When she did so, she saw "two angels in white" (v. 12). One of the angels asked

Mary why she was weeping; she responded by repeating her charge that Jesus's body has been "taken away" (v. 13).

It is at this point that one of the most wondrous moments in all of history unfolded. Mary turned around and saw a man there, though she thought little of him. In one of the Bible's most remarkable short phrases, in this confused moment, John records that Mary was "supposing him to be the gardener" (v. 15).

I believe that this tucked-away comment connects the threads discussed in this chapter. Humanity, as we have seen, was not made for the wilderness, for dry and parched ground, for sustained sojourn, for an exilic existence. Humanity was made for the safety and beauty of a garden. But while we lost the garden, we did not lose the Gardener.

In our sinful state, we are all like Mary. We are not looking for Jesus, and even when he is face to face with us, we do not recognize who he is. We do not naturally grasp the magnitude of Christ's nearness, nor rightly value the gift of his presence. Like Mary, we roam the earth, east of Eden, unsettled and lost.

But here is the marvelous truth. Though we do not hunt down Jesus, Jesus is out there looking for us. He is the agent of the Father's great love. He is the shepherd who leaves ninety-nine sheep to find just one (Matthew 18:12). Or, switching back to the context of John 20, Jesus is the gardener of his people. He does not live to condemn us; he lives to bless us, bring us to life, and bear much fruit through us.

Of course, Jesus was not technically the gardener of the area where Mary encountered him. But I believe it is not too much to conclude that John tucked a vital secret into this account. Jesus *is* the Gardener. By this I mean that he is the one who gives us the blessing that Adam and Eve first tasted in Eden. Jesus gives us rest—lasting *shalom,* which Philip Graham Ryken defines as "comprehensive peace."

Ryken expounds on the point: "Shalom means order, harmony, and happiness. It means that all is right with the city."[16] Shalom and rest are the gift of God, and each is found not in a certain location on earth, but in a person. Jesus said as much: if we come unto him, he will give us rest (see Matthew 11:29). We could put it this way: everything good in Eden is ours in Jesus.

To know the blessings of Eden you do not need to find a given location on earth. To find the blessings of Eden, you need only to meet a person, Jesus Christ the Gardener, and trust him as your Savior and Lord.

Conclusion

When we visit a beautiful garden, it transports us. We cannot help but be reminded, deep in our soul, of a similar place that we lost. At some level, every person has a lingering longing for a lush and living land, a place of rest. In this place, God walks with man. There, every good thing abounds, and no evil thing can enter.

As we saw in the Introduction, C. S. Lewis called this awareness of the far country *sehnsucht*; I have called it garden hunger. I felt this palpably when I visited a rock quarry turned retreat outside of Victoria in Western Canada. But I have not only felt longing; I have felt rest. Jesus, after all, is the one who gives what was lost in Eden: rest for our weary souls.

This gift does not breed laziness or laxness, though. It liberates us. The Christian is freed to grow our own gardens, to plant not only seeds, but faith and hope and love. Our entire life in Christ is a cultivating life. In this life, our hands dig deep into earth's soil, we honor God as servants in all that we do, and the sun of God's smile shines on our face.

CHAPTER 4

Create Families

The Joy of Deep Connection

Take wives and have sons and daughters; take wives for your sons, and give your daughters in marriage, that they may bear sons and daughters; multiply there, and do not decrease.

—Jeremiah 29:6

If you wanted to defeat the prince of darkness, you would likely turn to a fearsome force to do so. An army of angels. A legion of fearsome warriors. A tribe of wonder-working deliverers. You would assume that you can only fight fire with fire, after all. But in making this common assumption, you would be wrong.

To defeat sin, Satan, death, and hell, here is what you *actually* need: a young woman, great with child, bewildered by her new-found pregnancy, with a husband descended from the house of David. This is not what we would expect in terms of world-shaking action on God's part. But God loves to confound our expectations.

Throughout the Bible, he blesses his people by giving a childless woman the gift of pregnancy. So it was for forgotten Leah; Moses's godly mother; persevering Hannah; assertive Ruth; and, above all other examples, young Mary, betrothed to Joseph. Through these women came many of the most heroic leaders, warriors, and rescuers of the people of God. Before the spectacular, we could say, came the ordinary.

The lesson for us is plain: to accomplish his miraculous purposes, God does not depend on human strength. Instead, God uses what is weak to shame the mighty. To bring forward the Warrior-Savior of the world, God gave a young virgin the miracle of conception. The salvation of the world depended on God's unique blessing of the natural family.

The War over the Womb

It is not only the people of God who know this truth. Our great opponent also knows it. Ever since the Garden of Eden, Satan has been attacking the natural family. Satan hates the masterwork of God: humanity. He gave shape and form to this hatred in the Garden of Eden, declaring war on marriage, children, and the family most broadly.

The staging ground of the war between God and the devil was the family. This war has not stopped since. It continues into the present day. In recent decades, the American family has faced one challenge after another. Here are some modern trends that bode ill for the natural family:

- The average age of marriage has risen to 30 for men and 28 for women.

- In 2025, about 40 percent of first marriages end in divorce.[1]
- As of 2019, cohabitation rates nearly tripled, rising from 6 million to 17 million.[2]
- In 2024, the US fertility rate hit a record low with fewer than 1.6 kids per woman.[3]
- In recent years, 25 percent of 40-year-olds in the United States had never been married, rising from 20 percent in 2010.[4]
- In 2024, 9.3 percent of US adults identified as lesbian, gay, bisexual, transgender, or something other than heterosexual, a major increase from 3.5 percent in 2012.[5]
- As of 2025, over 63 million abortions have been performed in America since 1973.[6]

Taking these matters together, we see a clear narrative: the family is under fire today. Marriages are struggling. Children are hurting. Families are breaking apart. All this is sadly true. Yet here is a second truth: this is not a new phenomenon. Ever since Eden, the natural family has faced many challenges, and yet God has not given up on his beautiful design for humanity.

The Family Renewed

In ages past, instead of *relinquishing* the family, God has *renewed* the family. This is what God did with the people of Judah in the sixth century BC. Beleaguered, embattled, and burned out, they took up residence in Babylon. They likely felt like their exile meant death in all directions, including death to the dream of established lineage and stable homes.

But this was not what God had in mind. Though God rightly judged the sin of his people, he did not tell them to close up shop and stop having children. He did the opposite: he called his people to undertake the work of family-building once more. He made this unmistakably clear in Jeremiah 29:6, urging them to "Take wives and have sons and daughters; take wives for your sons, and give your daughters in marriage, that they may bear sons and daughters; multiply there, and do not decrease."

We cannot underscore how significant this reaffirmation of God's creational design was for the exiles. They had not come to Babylon to wither and die, as they might have wondered. They were not to fade away as so many ancient tribes did. God desired that the Judahites grow in Babylon, not be subsumed into Babylon. He wanted them to thrive in Babylon, even "multiply" in the foreign city.

This language strikingly echoes the original creation mandate of Genesis 1:28: "And God blessed them. And God said to them, 'Be fruitful and multiply and fill the earth and subdue it, and have dominion over the fish of the sea and over the birds of the heavens and over every living thing that moves on the earth.'"

The original call of God was to "multiply" across the earth. From the outset, we see that God has never put fear of resource scarcity or energy depletion in his peoples' minds. Even as the people filled the earth with children, God would fill the earth with plenty. Indeed, he had not made the earth to be evacuated and abandoned; he made the earth to be inhabited and enjoyed. A good

God made a "very good" creation for the blessing of families (see Genesis 1:31).

God did not reverse this mandate after the fall occurred. We might expect that he would do so, pulling the plug on his good intentions for humanity. Instead, he repeatedly blessed his people by enabling them to "multiply." This happened even in great hardship, as in the Egyptian captivity during the days of Moses (roughly 1450–1410 BC).

Despite severe treatment by the Egyptians, the people of God flourished in that place. In "a foreign land and under less than ideal conditions, Israel's numbers did in fact increase," as Jack Lundbom noted.[7] Though the people faced every human obstacle, God blessed them, nonetheless. He gave the Israelites many children, and their numbers grew so large that the Egyptians grew alarmed (see Exodus 1).

The Blessing of Marriage

As in Egypt, so God promised to do in Babylon. Wayward as his people were, straying as they often did, God had not sent them to Babylon to shrivel and die. Astonishingly, he had planted them in Babylon to flourish there and to bear much fruit—literally to bear so many children that the tribe of Judah *multiplied* in their exile.

It may well have been that the daughters and sons of the exiles reared back at the prospect of marriage. Perhaps they feared entering wedded life after all the difficulties of the fall of Israel and Judah. If this was true for them, we can surely understand why they might feel this way. But God nonetheless called fathers and mothers to help the next generation and guide their offspring into marriage.

The charge to "take wives for your sons, and give your daughters in marriage" reminds us that family-building is indeed a family affair. In the biblical mold, parents do not leave their children to figure things out, giving them neither guidance nor help. In the biblical mold, fathers and mothers bless the next generation by lovingly shepherding them and directing them toward the formation of future families.

We need not read into this a timeless call to arrange marriages for our children in a restrictive or suffocating way. What we hear instead is a summons to invest in the next generation by wise and gracious care. As fathers and mothers cultivated their own marriage and family, they would prepare the rising generation for the same, putting hope into practical form. Today, we can learn from their example, and do likewise in our confused age.

What Babylonian Families Were Like

As we do today, the exiles of Judah found themselves in a strange culture. They were called to build godly families side by side with the Babylonian family, dedicated to an entirely different worldview. In structural terms, the Babylonian family mirrored the Israelite family. Men functioned as the heads of their home and had the responsibility to provide for their loved ones.

The Babylonians treated family bonds with great seriousness. Extended families stayed close, often living side by side, and homes were handed down through generations. The Babylonian family centered in stability and tradition, with marriage between a man and a woman held in high regard. The spirituality of the Babylonian family showed real differences from God-centered homes, however.

Husbands could take a slave as a functional "secondary wife."[8] Furthermore, the Babylonian family found its identity in polytheistic religion, as the household worshiped many gods. In the case of the home, the gods Kabta and Mushdamma had spiritual oversight of the home construction process. Babylonians sought formal blessing of the home before building began, in fact, even as the god Arazu received thanks once construction finished.[9]

This material helps us illuminate what it was like to live in Babylon as an exile. Over against a vision of ancient peoples as disinterested earth-dwellers, the historical record reveals that the Babylonians were deeply religious. They saw all of life as spiritual and believed that a panoply of gods presided over everyday doings. The entire city, in fact, existed under the rule of the temple deity.

The populace served the will of the god in residence. This fact helps us understand why ancient wars were fought with such viciousness, and defeats experienced in such despair, in the ancient world. When one people conquered another, the outcome represented the defeat not only of an army, but an entire religion and way of life besides.

The Babylonians indulged the flesh as well. Society did not ban homosexual practice, and the goddess Inanna (or Ishtar) had the power to transform men into women and women into men. The religious leaders who served the will of Inanna were in many cases bisexual or gender-fluid (to use a modern term). Nor was this sexual liquidity known only in Babylon; across the ancient world, the goddesses Anat (of Assyria), Asherah (of Canaan), and Ishtar (of Persia) had similar qualities and encouraged similar behaviors.

We know for certain that some form of this sexual goddess influenced the people of Judah. According to the Prophet Jeremiah, the women of Judah made secret domestic offerings to "the queen of heaven" (see Jeremiah 7:18 and 44:15–19). They made little cakes bearing the image of the "queen" even as they poured out drink offerings to her.[10] The scholar J. A. Thompson sheds further light on this hidden idolatry:

> Whatever may have been the official religion of Israel, the women had indulged in a peculiarly women's kind of worship for centuries. . . . Such worship could remain hidden by its very nature, requiring only a pinch of incense, a libation, or a cake in the shape of a woman, crescent, or star (all symbols of Ishtar). . . . All this provoked Yahweh to anger.[11]

The condemnation of "the queen" shows us that God cares about the great and the small alike. He wanted the temple cleansed of idolatrous ceremonies just as he wanted pagan domestic rituals to cease.[12] It was this temptation, and not Babylonian militarism, that posed a grave threat to the Jews (and to us today). The key problem before the exiles was not that they lived in Babylon, but that Babylon lived in them.

The Hopeful Work of Family-Building

Jeremiah 29:6 reminds us of the distinctiveness of the people of God, then and now. In Babylon, the exiles were not to follow Inanna. They were not to worship household deities. They could not practice sexual fluidity. Anchored in God, they were instead charged to embrace family, flourishing, life-building, and witness: "Take wives and have sons and daughters; take wives for your sons, and give your daughters in marriage, that they may bear sons and daughters; multiply there, and do not decrease."

The Judahite exiles very likely may have felt that their deportation to Babylon meant their withering. God refuted this feeling in no uncertain terms: he wanted the remnant of his people to "multiply" in a hard place and a sinful society. But this life did not look sterile or joyless. God called them to a life of joy and satisfaction and hard work and investment. He called them to marry. Love life. Seek to have children. Multiply in Babylon.

God planted a new garden. It was the garden of the family, teeming with love and nurtured by the water of faith. Of course, God's words in Jeremiah 29 do not bind us today. But they do reflect how God wants us to live in the age of our own exile. As we have seen above, our context is marked by hostility to children, a propensity to divorce, an interest in sexual fluidity, and a tendency to cohabit. If we are going to build families in this context, we will need a strong biblical foundation for such work.

In what follows, here are five ways to build healthy families in our day.

First Way to Build Families: Be Distinct from Babylon

To be an exile in Babylon meant not acting in Baylon's patterns. Learning from their example, we New Covenant believers must stand apart from our fallen culture, wherever we live. We cannot buy into its worldview; we cannot adopt its mentality; we cannot mimic its practices; we cannot train our children in the catechism of culture. Toward this end, here are several truths we need to affirm and proclaim today.

There are only two sexes. Jesus affirms what Genesis declares: there are only two sexes. "He answered, 'Have you not read that he who created them from the beginning made them male and female'" (Matthew 19:4). This material shapes our understanding of humanity. We cannot embrace any vision of the human person that blurs these clear lines. In the world God has made, there are not many "gender identities." There are only men or women. No man has ever become a woman; no woman has ever become a man.

To the contrary, we are all made by God, and God has determined who we are. The sexes reflect God's wisdom, and we have the joyful opportunity to display God's glory as a redeemed man and a redeemed woman. In raising our children in modern Babylon, we stand apart from our culture's sexual confusion, raising masculine sons and feminine daughters.

God loves marriage. God holds marriage in high esteem. Jesus taught the goodness of marriage, honoring the original blueprint of God. When the Pharisees interrogated him about divorce, Jesus answered by citing Genesis 2:24.

> He answered, "Have you not read that he who created them from the beginning made them male and female, and said, 'Therefore a man shall leave his father and his mother and hold fast to his wife, and the two shall

> become one flesh'? So they are no longer two but one flesh. What therefore God has joined together, let not man separate." (Matthew 19:5–6)

As we see here, God defined marriage in Eden, and Jesus honored that design in his ministry. No software update is available for marriage. As it was in Eden, marriage brings one man together with one woman in covenantal union for life. This framework is not merely naturally good; it points beyond the domestic to the eternal. Marriage represents the loving bond between Christ the head and his bride the church (see Ephesians 5:22–33), a picture we honor and protect.

God forbids sexual desires and activities outside of marriage. God did not only design marriage. God designed sex, making it for marriage. Though the passage makes many a youth-group hearer blush when it is read aloud, Genesis 2:25 indicates that Adam and Eve had no shame in naked sexual union. Shame came through the fall, not through the original plan of God.

The fall warped our sexual instincts. I do not mean only our behavior; I mean our very desires. Romans 1:24–27 connects evil sexual desire to godless sexual action.

> [Therefore] God gave them up in the lusts of their hearts to impurity, to the dishonoring of their bodies among themselves, because they exchanged the truth about God for a lie and worshiped and served the creature rather than the Creator, who is blessed forever! Amen.

Sexual sin comes not from a vacuum but from "the lusts" of our "hearts," as Paul puts it. All of this reminds us that there is only one form of sexual interest and action that God has blessed. It is sex with—and sexual desire for—one's spouse.[13] No other pattern of behavior or desire honors God. Today, sexual desire is seen as good provided it springs from you "authentically." But Scripture does not affirm this view; the New Testament clearly distinguishes godly sexual desire from godless sexual desire.

Second Way to Build Families: Embrace a Biblical Vision of Marriage

A healthy marriage takes a "complementarian" shape. The sexes do not compete with one another; the sexes "complement" one another.[14] A godly man honors the wisdom and ability of a godly woman, just as a godly woman welcomes the wise and self-sacrificial authority of a godly man. In relational terms, biblical womanhood looks like godliness, dignity, trust, and service, and biblical manhood looks like gentleness, kindness, self-sacrifice, and respect toward women.

In Scripture, men are called by God to lead in both the home and the church. This is unequivocally true in the biblical witness (see Ephesians 5:22–33; 1 Timothy 2:9–15; 3:1–7). However, the reality of our sin and distortions of the truth necessitate that we think with great care about what godly leadership is and is not.

Our culture has pushed back sharply against men as leaders and women as nurturers. Men have been told, in fact, to "lean back," while women have received much encouragement to transcend domesticity by embracing careerism. This "egalitarian" conception of marriage does not reflect Scripture's teaching, nor will it enable the sexes to flourish as God intends. Again, God's design is for loving complementarity, in which men honor the gifts and role of women, and women honor the gifts and role of men.

But "egalitarianism" is not our only challenge today. At present, in Christian and conservative circles, there is a rising tide of young men and women who want to reject weak masculinity and godless feminism. They want to practice "trad marriage." Some say they reject feminism and now embrace "patriarchy." Some drawn to these models say things like the following:

- The sexes are flatly "unequal," and women are "inferior" to men.
- Since women don't think well, men should make decisions autonomously.
- Men rule their wives as their superiors and should demand obedience from them.
- Girls need not develop or think outside of the calling of a wife and mother (college is wasteful for them).
- It is a duty for women to have as many children as humanly possible.
- Men should not apologize to their families because that would "weaken their authority."
- The emotional nature of women means that they do not think well.
- Women need not vote or have any vocal role in church or society, as that would oppose male leadership.

- Headship means men are "pastors" of their homes and so are obligated to lead family worship on a daily basis.[15]

I have no doubt that some who hold these views do so with good intentions. However, I also believe that the above ideals need—to varying degrees—some rounding out, some refining. It is simply untrue that men and women are "unequal," and that women are "inferior" to men. The man was made first, and the woman was made from his body (Genesis 2). However, both the man and the woman bear the image of God.

In dignity and worth, the sexes are equal before God. Their bodies, gifting, and roles will differ in numerous respects; some things men do better, and some things women do better. This truth is no threat to the personhood of either sex. But the sexes are of equal value and equal necessity. One sex is not "superior" to the other; in biblical complementarity, the sexes fit together, work together, and glorify God together.

Of course, there is surely an order to biblical marriage. According to Scripture, a godly woman honors and even obeys her husband as Sarah did (1 Peter 3:6). However, a godly husband does not treat his wife like a child or a second-class citizen. To the contrary, 1 Peter 3:7 calls husbands to "live with your wives in an understanding way, showing honor to the woman as the weaker vessel, since they are heirs with you of the grace of life, so that your prayers may not be hindered."

The woman is likened to a "weaker vessel," and elsewhere Paul identifies Eve as susceptible to deception (1 Timothy 2:14). This does not entail, however, that women are hyper-gullible, foolish, or unable to think straight because of their complex emotional nature. It means instead that a woman's capacity for compassion must be guarded by her husband. He is her protector, even as her leader and provider.

He offers this protection not to an inferior, but to the woman who is a co-heir of God's grace. This shapes all his headship of his wife and his leadership in the home. A godly man is a leader, and he is responsible before God for providing actual on-the-ground leadership in the home. He makes decisions, he works out solutions, he makes plans for the good of his family, and he provides spiritual guidance and strength to his family.

But his leadership is not normally one of kingly ultimatums. His is a loving authority. He is a strong man, but he is a kind man. He is a brave man, but he is a gentle man. He is a fearless man, but he is a tender man. He is not perfect by a long shot, but he seeks to grow in these godly attributes over the course of his marriage. He treats his wife with kindness, gentleness, and understanding, and in this way "nourishes" and "cherishes" her (see Ephesians 5:29).

A godly man is a blend of conviction and humility. He leads his family in worship, but does so in a relaxed way, unbound by commandments of men. As mentioned, he is called by God to make decisions for his family, but he does so in a way that solicits his wife's wisdom, invites her counsel, and encourages her feedback. He leads with courage, and his godly wife supports him. But when he sins and gets things wrong, he leads in confession. He repents of wrongdoing, humbly asks for forgiveness, and strives to make right what has gone wrong.

A godly wife honors such a man. She does not treat him like an idiot or a second-class citizen. She submits to him, seeking to walk in "respectful and pure conduct" (1 Peter 2:2). She may have an outgoing personality or a quiet one, but either way she prays to be clothed "with the imperishable beauty of a gentle and quiet spirit" (v. 4). She delights in her home and her family.

In fact, she does not see biblical womanhood as *squelching* her God-given gifts. Rather, as modeled in the woman of Proverbs 31, she sees biblical womanhood as *summoning* her unique skills and abilities. In that mindset, she nurtures her environment and her family, bringing her children and her home itself to a place of flourishing, stability, and delight as God allows.

The sexes are not the same. But in a marriage anchored in the gospel, they do not compete with one another, striving in an ongoing Domestic Sweepstakes Battle to crown one sex as the victor over the other. They complement one another. A godly husband builds up a godly wife; a godly wife builds up a godly husband. Their foundation is God; their goal is growth; their union is love.

Third Way to Build Families: Cultivate a Gospel-Driven Marriage

In truth, it takes a great deal of hard work to develop a healthy, God-glorifying marriage. But we must take care not to be discouraged here: for most Christians, marriage is a major way we grow in godliness. It is one of the most effective tools of sanctification that God wields in our lives, and God does not only use it for an afternoon or a week. Over the long haul, with many fits and starts, through the rough and the smooth, God changes us.

In my twentieth year of marriage, I can honestly say that the preceding paragraphs are true. I am married to a woman I adore. She is a blessing to me in every way one can measure. She makes a killer scone, she works tirelessly with our kids in their daily schooling, and she fills our home with beauty and life. Above all, my wife is godly, a woman who lives to glorify God in every way she can.

Marriage has grown us a great deal. There is much I could list out here, but at base, I have learned in two decades of marriage this lesson above all: I need the gospel. In fact, I need the gospel for my marriage (and my whole life) more than I need oxygen. Here are three ways the gospel has helped me as a husband.

First, the gospel has freed me to admit that I get things wrong. If I am honest, I have never liked admitting that I was wrong. Once, in a moment of particular hard-heartedness, I actually shouted at a coach in basketball practice when he rightly called me out on an error. I am not sure who was more shocked by my outburst: him or me!

Thankfully, God has jack-hammered up my stubborn heart. It has taken years for me to grow in this, and I wish I could say that I grew faster than I have. However, despite my slowness of progress, I can look back and say that God has clearly exposed and addressed my sin, as marriage tends to do. God has graciously helped me see that humility and repentance are not signs of weakness. Humility and repentance are signs of spiritual strength—the work of God in us.

Second, the gospel has helped me to forgive. Marriages get jammed up by a failure to confess sin, owning it honestly, but also by a failure to forgive. Here is good news: the gospel frees us to forgive generously. This is why Christian marriage is so distinct: it is based in the good news of God forgiving our sin through the blood of Christ.

With this as our spiritual foundation, we are liberated from the instinct to choose bitterness over grace. We who have been forgiven much need to forgive much. We also, at times, simply need to move on. Marriages can get bogged down, stuck in the mud of a hard decision, a tough week, or a time of stress. To get unstuck, we need to practice forgiveness, bite our tongue, and move on with our day. Proverbs says it well: "Good sense makes one slow to anger, and it is his glory to overlook an offense" (Proverbs 19:11).

Third, the gospel has enabled me to embrace self-denying servanthood. Christian marriage anchored in the gospel creates a servant mindset. This does not mean that you become a robot; it does mean that you spend great energy and effort working for the good of your spouse. You structure your whole life to bless them and give them joy.

Putting someone before you means much death to self. It means that you do not always get what you want, nor often push for what you want. (It also means that you fail at this and have to repent of such failure throughout your life!) Of course, this does not entail that a spouse never communicates their needs or desires; in a healthy marriage, couples communicate a great deal.

In a gospel-driven marriage, each spouse seeks the good of the other above their own self-interest. They do not expect functional perfection of their spouse; rather, they recognize that God uses both the strengths and weaknesses of their spouse for their own growth. Paul Washer says it well:

> How would you ever learn unconditional love if you were married to someone who met all the conditions? How would you ever learn mercy, patience, long-suffering, heart-felt compassion if you were married to someone who never failed you? Who is never difficult with you? Who never sinned against you? Who is never slow to acknowledge their sin or ask for forgiveness? How would you ever learn grace, to pour out your favor on someone who did not deserve it, if you were married to someone who was always deserving of all good things? The main purpose of marriage is that through your marriage, you both become conformed to the image of Jesus Christ.[16]

Fourth Way to Build Families: Guide Our Children

As we have seen in Jeremiah 29:6, God envisioned that a godly couple would lead in family-building. In practical form, this meant that they would help their sons and daughters to find a spouse. Today, when the script for maturity seems lost for many young people, we do well to hear God's word to the Babylonian exiles afresh and help our children gain wisdom about marriage.

The best preparation for our children to have a healthy marriage is by witnessing a healthy marriage. Beyond this foundation, we can do a number of things to build a marriage pathway for our children who are called to it.

First, we can present marriage (as with singleness) as a godly calling. We can speak well of marriage, commend it to our children, and frame biblical and practical expectations for a godly union.

Second, we can offer calm leadership as they mature. As time goes on and our child hits the teenage years, a godly father and mother offer gracious oversight of their child's social life. They honor their interest in the opposite sex but steer it wisely. In general, it is good to have more communication about these matters rather than less. We want our children to feel like they can come to us, talk honestly with us, and have our help to figure out the wilds of adolescence.

Third, we can help them pursue purity. This pursuit does not reduce to a set of legalistic rules. While we will surely put wise guidelines and even guardrails in place, we center all our pursuit of purity in the gospel. We help our children understand that sex is God's good gift, but like all good gifts, it has to be stewarded well and ordered by God's design.

Fourth, when our children are of age, we can encourage them to move forward. The New Testament does not give us a step-by-step manual for entering marriage. This means that a Christian father and mother have freedom in how they handle the romantic prospects of their children. They are free to suggest possible interests and to facilitate interaction in a healthy, balanced way.

Fifth, churches can also offer some structure and encouragement to young people desiring marriage. Some young men and women—let's say of college age—may not have parental support here. It's very important to look not only to the natural family for help, but the spiritual family. Churches should play a role in helping young people find the pathway to marriage. This need not be overly formal or programmed, but it is a good thing in my book when churches set up opportunities through "college and career ministries" and the like for young people to meet each other.

Sixth, we can practice a balanced approach to romance called "dateship." In this approach, when a young man has interest in a young woman, he asks her father (or a church leader) for permission to get to know her in a godly way. They go on some dates, and hang out with friends and church members in a relaxed way. If things progress, he asks for permission to court her, beginning a season when the couple prays over the real prospect of marriage. If the Lord leads him toward her, he asks her father (or a church leader) for her hand in marriage, and waits for her response.

This is not a foolproof system. It is merely one attempt, framed by Christian liberty, to give some shape to a romantic culture that has lost clarity in our sexually "liberated" culture. Today, there are no "rules" or script by which young people approach marriage. This is not a good situation. We have freedom to fill in the details here, but I sense that many young people need some godly but relaxed help in avoiding the pitfalls of modern "romance."

Fifth Way to Build Families: Honor the Spiritual Family

Sometimes I hear Christian leaders suggest that maturing to adulthood equals getting married. For many young people, this rings true. They need marriage, and they should pursue marriage. But for others, maturity does not equal marriage. In 1 Corinthians 7:8, the Apostle Paul commends godly singleness. He goes so far as to pronounce it "good" to stay single: "To the unmarried and the widows I say that it is good for them to remain single, as I am."

In 1 Corinthians 7:32–34, he expands on this teaching. Paul regards single people as "anxious about the things of the Lord" (v. 32). By this he means that godly singleness creates untold opportunities to serve Christ. Single men and women do not need to think for a second about how to please a spouse. They can dedicate themselves to God, to evangelism and missions, and to the body of Christ.

In this way, we see that Scripture honors what I call "doxological singleness"—a single man or woman using their God-given gifts to praise their Creator and Savior. Such believers do not live apart from family; they belong with every Christian to a much bigger family than their own, as we have seen. This is the true family, the family of God, defined by Jesus: "For whoever does the will of my Father in heaven is my brother and sister and mother" (Matthew 12:50).

The natural family is good and important in the kingdom of Jesus. It is not dissolved in the New Covenant; the natural family endures in this age. But even as the natural family matters in many ways, we must never forget that there is a family far greater than the natural family. It is the spiritual family, made one "household of God" by the blood of Christ (Ephesians 2:19). In this family, we are all one—married and single alike.

Conclusion

God has staked a great deal on the family. In fact, nothing less than the salvation of the world comes through the ordinary work of childbirth. To save us, God did not send a legion of angels, nor a host of warriors. To save us, God gave an unsuspecting young woman the gift of pregnancy. In this way, God affirmed the natural family even as he showed us that it is not sufficient to redeem us. God used natural means in a supernatural way, giving conception to Mary by the Holy Spirit.

The Virgin Conception shows us that God loves marriage, and God loves the family. All throughout biblical history, God reaffirmed this principle. He did so in surprising moments, not the least of them the exile to Babylon. He called them to "multiply" in Babylon, to embrace the abundance and vitality of the family, and to build marriages centered in him that would testify to the goodness of God.

In our own modern Babylon, we do well to hear this ancient call. We live in an era when paganism thrives once more. An antihuman ethic poisons the land. A counterfeit sexuality has arisen in our age. In such a time, we should do something both extraordinary and altogether normal: build families. Strengthen our marriages. Look to the future, and take wives for our sons, and give our daughters in marriage, trusting in the God who loves life, and loves the family.

CHAPTER 5

Seek Shalom

The Power of Loving Witness

But seek the welfare of the city where I have sent you into exile, and pray to the LORD on its behalf, for in its welfare you will find your welfare.
—Jeremiah 29:7

When I am not writing books and working on theology projects, I have another role in life: amateur basketball coach. Actually, in technical terms, amateur homeschool basketball coach. I sometimes think to myself, driving to practice, that I may just be the absolute lowest rung on the ladder of all basketball coaches in America.

But this humorous musing masks a greater reality: I absolutely love coaching. It is one of the most enjoyable endeavors God has given man to do, I believe. For this reason, over the last few years, I have had the great joy—and undeserved privilege—of coaching my son's basketball teams. It has actually provided me with my own little experience in employing a *cultivation* mindset. I love seeing these young men develop, gain confidence, and make friendships.

There are some funny moments, too. If you've ever tried to coach—or teach kids most anything—you know of what I speak. With thirty seconds to go, I call a time-out and draw up a makeshift play, asking my players to stall the clock. We inbound the ball and promptly throw the ball out of bounds. Coaching is humbling, I have learned, and you never know quite what you will get.

This tendency is not found only among testosterone-fueled young athletes, of course. It's *human*. How often have we said a comment when we should have remained silent? How frequently have we remained silent when we should have spoken up? We have a disconcerting tendency to do the opposite of what is best.

This is not a new problem, but an ancient one. In the Old Testament, God's followers regularly heard God's instructions and then did the opposite. Here are three sin patterns of God's people in ages past, patterns that recur today.

The Instinct to Accommodate

We have seen already in these pages that Judah accommodated the sins of surrounding cultures, embracing them as their own. The book of Jeremiah indicts just this kind of failure in scorching terms:

> Behold, you trust in deceptive words to no avail. Will you steal, murder, commit adultery, swear falsely, make offerings to Baal, and go after other gods that you have not known, and then come and stand before me in this house, which is called by my name, and say, "We are delivered!"—only to go on doing all these abominations? Has this house, which is called by my name, become a

> den of robbers in your eyes? Behold, I myself have seen it, declares the LORD. (Jeremiah 7:8–11)

The wicked actions of Judah triggered the Babylonian exile, as we have seen. At the root of this godless action: "trust in deceptive words" (v. 8). The people of Judah did not trust God; they chose to trust in other voices. They put their faith in other rulers, not in their Redeemer.

The Judahites longed to act according to the flesh. In the religions around them, they found a worldview that enabled them to do just that. As they made "offerings to Baal" and chased "other gods that you have not known," they lost their inhibitions and gained an immoral nerve. They felt justified in a panoply of perversity, stealing, killing, committing adultery, breaking their word left and right, and—most shocking of all—pronouncing themselves delivered by God in the temple.

The wickedness of the people reached still further. As Jeremiah 7:30–31 substantiates, the remnant of Judah went so far into pagan practice that they sacrificed their offspring to false gods. Words scarcely capture the depth of evil of this behavior:

> For the sons of Judah have done evil in my sight, declares the LORD. They have set their detestable things in the house that is called by my name, to defile it. And they have built the high places of Topheth, which is in the Valley of the Son of Hinnom, to burn their sons and their daughters in the fire, which I did not command, nor did it come into my mind.

None of this conduct came from God. God did not "command" it nor did such evil sully his "mind." Pagan worship dedicated to "detestable things" in the temple and in "the high places" brought out an especially nasty form of idolatry: the killing of Judah's sons and daughters by fire.

This was not an uncommon practice in the ancient world. In a ritual sacrifice elsewhere, the god Kronos (akin to Baal) received children unto death. The Greek historian Diodorus Siculus wrote the following of the rite: "There was in the city a bronze image of Kronos, extending its hands, palms up and sloping toward the ground, so that each of the children when placed thereon rolled down and fell into a sort of gaping pit filled with fire" (*Bibliotheca*, book xx, chapter 14).[1]

Instead of being a light in the world, Judah became like the nations. In doing so, the people turned on their own children. Their action was as symbolically rich as it was morally abhorrent: they destroyed the next generation. They left themselves with no familial inheritance. In the face of such evil, Jeremiah called the people of Judah to stop their approach of cultural *accommodation*. Turning from this sin was the only way out and the only way forward.

The Instinct to Attack

The people of God did not only *accommodate* the nations, however. At different points, they foolishly disobeyed the call of God by taking matters into their own hands and trying to battle their way out of their self-caused difficulties. Far from God and no longer listening to his voice, they wrongly thought that they could solve their problems by conquering foreign peoples.

Of course, earlier in the story of God's people, God did indeed call his chosen to war. God did not urge Joshua to take Canaan, the promised land, by sending the Canaanites and Amorites bouquets of roses. He called the twelve tribes of Israel to go and fight for the land promised to them (see Joshua 1). This was a righteous call.

But this program of war had long since concluded by the days of Jeremiah. The people of Judah heard no call to arms. Under the righteous rule of Josiah, they found themselves in a difficult place, caught between rival powers. As Babylon and Egypt vied for rule in the Middle East, Josiah stayed out of the conflict, enacting widespread reform in Judah.

Over the course of his thirty-one-year reign (640–609), Josiah pushed back much of the evil that had overtaken the southern kingdom. Under Josiah's leadership, Hilkiah the priest found the Book of the Law and brought it to Josiah (see 2 Kings 22:8). Shaphan read it to Josiah, and Josiah immediately responded in grief and repentance before the Lord (vv. 14–19).

Josiah did not stop there; he engaged the prophetess Huldah to learn more about the will of God (vv. 22–28). The Lord commended Josiah for his action: "because your heart was responsive and you humbled yourself before God when you heard what he spoke against this place and its people, and because you humbled yourself before me and tore your robes and wept in my presence, I have heard you, declares the Lord" (2 Chronicles 34:26–28).

God delighted in Josiah's "responsive" heart, one sensitive to his truth and his holiness. Living in God's blessing, Josiah recovered the role of Scripture in the life of Judah. The king renewed the covenant with the Lord in the Jerusalem temple, reading the words of the Book of the Covenant to the people. Once again, the Word of God assumed pride of place in Judah, just as God intended.

Josiah then struck back against pagan priests and false worship. He had all idolatrous items taken out of the temple and destroyed. So Josiah did with the high places, sites of the grossest pagan worship practices. They included the Asherah pole, where evil priests oversaw depraved sexual rites. Josiah sacked all of this, even as he celebrated the Passover once more in Jerusalem (see 2 Chronicles 35:1–3). He strengthened the hand of the Levites, making them central in worship of God as in older days. From top to bottom, Josiah transformed Judah through the gracious working of God.

Then Josiah did something altogether mystifying. Despite all the blessing God poured out upon Judah in the days of Josiah, Josiah decided that he should fight Pharoah Necho of Egypt. This behavior was so uncharacteristic, so foolish, that the Egyptian king took the unusual step of reaching out to Josiah, urging him not to fight (see 2 Chronicles 35:20–22). Josiah did not listen. He went to war and died on the battlefield that day. The southern kingdom, so powerfully revived, would shortly fade and crumble.

The man of a thousand good decisions made a single disastrous one. What a sobering reminder we glean from Josiah's example. Just one action we commit can upend years and even decades of God's blessing seen in our faithfulness. In Josiah's case, he chose the wrong approach. He wrongly thought he should attack, when wisdom demanded a much calmer course.

In his death, a heavy burden of grief fell upon Jeremiah and many others after Josiah fell. In Jeremiah 22:10, the prophet memorialized the godly king. "Weep not for him who is dead, nor grieve for him, but weep bitterly for him who goes away, for he shall return no more to see his native land." The bitterness of this grief still speaks, for Judah never saw a king like Josiah take the throne again. His instinct to attack led Judah into its final spiral of decline.

The Instinct to Abandon

Alongside accommodation of godlessness and a desire to attack and overcome foreign powers, the people of Judah yearned to exit Babylon. They wanted to abandon their place of exile, leaving it and never coming back. A willing audience created a market demand. As God carried out judgment against Judah for its sins, numerous false prophets arose to speak delusions of escape to the remnant.

In the simplest terms, these "prophets" did what charlatans have always done: they told the people what they wanted to hear. The Prophet Jeremiah had the lonely calling of correcting these false prophecies numerous times (see Jeremiah 23:16–17 and 27:16–22, for example). This challenge came to a head when Jeremiah went toe-to-toe with a false prophet named Hananiah.

Though Jeremiah had made clear to Judah collectively that its exile would last many decades—seventy years overall—Hananiah dared to challenge Jeremiah before the rulers and priests of Judah. Here was his false prophecy, offered (blasphemously) in the name of God:

> Thus says the LORD of hosts, the God of Israel: I have broken the yoke of the king of Babylon. Within two

> years I will bring back to this place all the vessels of the LORD's house, which Nebuchadnezzar king of Babylon took away from this place and carried to Babylon. I will also bring back to this place Jeconiah the son of Jehoiakim, king of Judah, and all the exiles from Judah who went to Babylon, declares the LORD, for I will break the yoke of the king of Babylon. (Jeremiah 28:2–4)

Hananiah used striking language to assure the exiles of their release, putting words in God's mouth: "I will break the yoke of the king of Babylon." This gave a faithless people just what they wanted: the ability to escape their exile. Jeremiah had no choice but to refute this false prophet, though he first honored the desire of the people to see Judah's glory restored. "Amen! May the LORD do so; may the LORD make the words that you have prophesied come true, and bring back to this place from Babylon the vessels of the house of the LORD, and all the exiles," Jeremiah responded (28:6).

Jeremiah knew that his words would put him in the penalty box with Hananiah's audience. Undaunted, he then issued a challenge to Hananiah directly: "As for the prophet who prophesies peace, when the word of that prophet comes to pass, then it will be known that the LORD has truly sent the prophet" (Jeremiah 28:9). In response, Hananiah doubled down. He reinforced the forcefulness of divine action that would free Judah: "Thus says the LORD: Even so will I break the yoke of Nebuchadnezzar king of Babylon from the neck of all the nations within two years" (v. 11).

Soon the Lord gave Jeremiah his own heavenly response to all this fluttery flattery:

> "For thus says the LORD of hosts, the God of Israel: I have put upon the neck of all these nations an iron yoke to serve Nebuchadnezzar king of Babylon, and they shall serve him, for I have given to him even the beasts of the field." And Jeremiah the prophet said to the prophet Hananiah, "Listen, Hananiah, the LORD has not sent you, and you have made this people trust in a lie. Therefore thus says the LORD: 'Behold, I will remove you from the face of the earth. This year you shall die, because you have uttered rebellion against the LORD.'" In that same year, in the seventh month, the prophet Hananiah died. (Jeremiah 28:14–17)

All of Hananiah's "prophesying" came to nothing. God did not throw off the yoke of Babylon from Judah's neck; God specified that he himself had raised up Nebuchadnezzar, and no man could—for that appointed time—conquer the Babylonian king. God went further: he had not sent Hananiah, the people had put the faith "in a lie" from this wicked man, and God silenced Hananiah through death.

There is much to learn here. Notably, God did not grant the wish of his feckless followers. God had put the exiles in Babylon for many decades, and nothing they could do could change this reality. The right reaction to God's leading was acceptance, not abandonment. But just as we do, the people of God struggled mightily to hear from God and obey what he said.

Aerating: The Call to Cultivate

Thus far, we have seen what God did not call his people to by way of mission. His plan for them was not to *accommodate* Babylon, embracing its sin as Judah sadly had already done. His plan for them was not to *attack* Babylon, going to war with it on an actual battlefield. Nor was his plan for them to *abandon* Babylon, posting up in a nicely furnished townhome for several months before heading swiftly back to Jerusalem.

The people of Judah wanted each of these outcomes at different times. In fact, they did everything they humanly could to bring these plans of theirs to pass. As we witness their efforts, we do not critique them from a high and lofty place, snorting at their faithless failures. We recognize in their foolish attempts to play God our own self-willed endeavors. We too want life to play out on our own timetable, not God's; we too want our plan to operate, not God's; we too want an easy existence, not a challenging one.

For headstrong types like us and like Judah of old, you would expect God to throw up his hands. You would think that his patience would end and he himself would either attack us or abandon us. But Yahweh did no such thing. He called his people back to the mission he gave them for their good and his glory. His mission was not to accommodate, attack, or abandon Babylon; his mission was to *aerate* Babylon.

What exactly, you might ask, is *aeration*? An unusual word borrowed from the world of gardening, aeration is the perforation of soil with small holes to allow air, water and nutrients to penetrate the grass roots. This practice (often with lawns, but with grass or land in general) enables nutrients to infuse the soil as air and water reach into layers of grass not easily reached.

The physical, I believe, closely tracks with the spiritual. In Jeremiah 29:7, we hear a call to *aerate* the spiritual soil of the fallen city, Babylon: "But seek the welfare of the city where I have sent you into exile, and pray to the LORD on its behalf, for in its welfare you will find your welfare." A close synonym for *aeration* is a word that we have used already in this book: *cultivation.*

In the simplest terms, the exiles of Judah were to bless Babylon. They were to do so by bringing the *shalom* of God's truth to it like nutrients spreading through parched land. This was no part-time mission, either; it was the central calling of the exiles. In their decades of residence in Babylon, they were to "seek the welfare of the city" in every way possible.

I cannot stress how transformative this call of God was. In the history of God's mission on earth, this verse—as with this passage—represents a remarkable turn. Once, God *did* call his people to conquer other peoples. Once, God did lead the people away from Egypt, no longer to reside there. But in this instance, God debuted a new wrinkle in his mission to rescue sinners. He called his people not out of Babylon, but into it.

The people balked at this mandate. Commentator Philip Ryken summarizes how they likely felt:

> No doubt when the captives discussed their sojourn in Babylon they used words like "abandoned" or "banished" or "condemned" to describe what God had done to them. But that is not how God saw things. He viewed

> the exile as a mission. Literally what he said was, "Seek the peace and prosperity of the city to which I have *sent* you." Nebuchadnezzar did not take them to Babylon. God sent them there. The exiles were not captives—they were missionaries.[2]

Ryken captures the essence of the Babylonian exile. It felt like captivity, but it was in truth missiology. The Jews were there, to use later biblical language, to be "salt and light" in it. They were not in Babylon to overthrow it; they were there to be the distinctive presence of godliness in it, a presence that would influence, affect, and in some ways transform it.

The Significance of the Call to Cultivate

The "plant gardens" mandate centered in cultivating Babylon for its own *shalom* forms a pivotal shift in biblical history, and all history besides. The erudite scholar Derek Kidner comments on the striking mandate placed before the people: "Even the New Testament, with its instructions to overcome evil with good and to 'adorn the doctrine of God' by 'by perfect courtesy toward all,' hardly outstrips the boldness of this teaching."[3]

Kidner is correct. Seeking the *shalom* of Babylon was unparalleled. No longer would the followers of God take up arms against pagan peoples in order to advance the cause of God. Now they would seek the good of pagan peoples by offering holy and loving witness to them on their very own turf. The people of God would actively pursue the good of these lost souls, not merely residing in a lost place, but planning and plotting and praying to see it changed for the better.

This fruitful labor does not simply encourage us. It helps us understand our own God-glorifying efforts in the era of the New Covenant, and it does so with tremendous insight. In what follows, we will trace what "seeking Babylon's shalom" meant for the remnant of Judah, connecting their mission to our witness today in six clear forms.

First, the Exiles Blessed Babylon by Fearing God

As we have seen, Judah had no call from God to become like Babylon. Though placed in Babylon, God desired that his people serve as a witness to his glory in the city. Judah struggled greatly with this charge, but that reality did not lessen the need for the exiles to worship God in a pagan place. The exiles had not landed in Babylon by accident, we recall. God wanted the remnant of his people to seek the good of the city by being a living witness in it.

A key part of this was being a good citizen in Babylon. The Jews were to live godly and upright lives, of course, but they were in every way to seek the good of Babylon. Veteran exegetes Walter Kaiser and Tiberius Rata point out that "This is more than mere prudential or pragmatic talk, for in doing so the people of Judah demonstrate they are once again the means by which God will bless all the nations of the earth."[4]

This was a comprehensive mandate, not a limited one. In all respects, God summoned Judah to bring *shalom* to a lost context. This meant being a good neighbor, living peacefully with others, bettering the community, investing in friendships, witnessing everywhere one could, making vocational contributions to the city, and much more. All this would bring *shalom* to Babylon. So it was that the "revolutionary message" of Jeremiah 29:4–7 would yield ordinary cultivation.[5] The supernatural would infuse the everyday, giving God glory.

The exiles' mandate mirrors ours today: we should not amend our faith to the world. We should not accommodate lies. Instead, we should fear God and live for his glory. If we wish to be a witness in our community and nation, we can only do so by remaining genuinely Christian. Too often, however, we think that we can reach Babylon (so to speak) by emulating Babylon. But this is not right: we need to reach Babylon by emulating heaven. To put it differently, we need to bring heaven to Babylon.

Second, the Exiles Blessed Babylon by Praying for It

The exiles of Judah were to bless Babylon. A major part of how they would do this was to pray for it. This is what verse 7 says explicitly about Babylon: *pray to the LORD on its behalf.* The people of God were not to pray *against* Babylon, in other words. Shockingly, the people of God were to pray *for* Babylon.

It is difficult to underplay how radical this call to prayer was. Scholar Jack R. Lundbom notes this about such a call from God: "Prayer for the welfare of a foreign (= heathen) nation is a radical idea in the OT," a claim we have seen borne out in this book already.[6] Philip Ryken concurs, observing that "Jeremiah 29:7 is the only verse in the entire Old Testament in which God's people are explicitly told to pray for their enemies."

We can go even further still. According to Ryken, this prayer is nothing other than "a foretaste of the forgiveness of Jesus Christ."[7] It is not a mere gesture of good faith, in other words.

Praying for Babylon means asking God to work in a fallen place to save sinners and unleash the power of his gospel. This is the opposite of praying for God to destroy the enemies of God; it represents a very different instinct than the righteous imprecatory prayers of Psalms (35, 59, 69, 109, and 137), for example.

But this is precisely what Yahweh called for. He directed prayers to himself for the advancement of Babylon's *shalom*. His charge is indeed a "radical" one; this commandment marks a transition in the life of God's people. No longer were they to pray against Babylon; now they were to pray for it. So should we in our own context.

Third, the Exiles Blessed Babylon by Proclaiming God's Mercy

The people of God were not in Babylon to overtake it. They were not a stealth presence to spy out how to overthrow it. They were not a sleeper cell to be activated when a signal went up, calling the Judahites to rise up and rebel against their Babylonian neighbors.

The people of God were sent to Babylon for something much more revolutionary than this. They were, as we saw in the previous point, to seek the good of Babylon. This was deeply surprising to the exiles of Judah, as we have noted throughout this chapter. The ancient world was a bone-crunching world. It was a place of exceedingly great danger and exceedingly little mercy. Unlike in our day, a Christian ethic had not influenced the pagan peoples of the Middle East. They sought to defeat, kill, and enslave one another, and they showed little kindness to those they conquered.

Further, ancient nations, after all, were not nearly so religiously chaste as many countries today. For one group to conquer another meant, quite directly, that one group of deities conquered another. All this was championed at home by a raft of idolatrous priests and a populace awash in polytheism.[8] Paganism went hand in glove with militarism. Indeed, it is not as though pagan nations played Foosball against one another. They sought to dominate one another, destroy one another, and altogether crush one another.

It was in this markedly lost context that God placed his people. He did not ask them to attack Babylon; he called his people to live in Babylon for its good. We can infer from this that Yahweh wanted the exiles to show the Babylonians what mercy looked like. The Babylonians, after all, lacked much in the area of mercy, as every tribe that is unreached does. In a kill-or-be-killed world, it is not natural to show compassion, kindness, and spiritual concern to others, then or now.

Mercy can take on many forms. At base, mercy means not giving people what they deserve (where grace means giving people what they do not deserve). Jeremiah 29 does not spell out what mercy might look like among the exiles as they bring it to bear on Babylon. But the very presence of the remnant of Judah in Babylon was itself a sign of great mercy on the part of God toward the Babylonians.

The greatest need of every person on earth is God's truth, God's redemption, and God's blessing. Now, because God had sent his people into Babylon, this lost people could come into contact with the saving work of God. They had long lived in darkness; now they could witness the light of God. Further, they could observe and be impacted by a life shaped by God's mercy. Kindness to one's enemies, again, is not natural. But wherever saving faith is found, kindness and goodness and forgiveness will crop up as well.

This speaks to our own calling. For our purposes, it is enough to note that just as the exiles of Judah brought *shalom* to Babylon, so we bring the healing of the gospel to our own community. Mercy toward sinners is always grounded in gospel proclamation and loving engagement; from there, it will take many forms, as believers find all sorts of ways to bless those around them. Those who are loved by God go on, in the Spirit's power, to love fellow sinners.

As just one example of this, I think of how the missionary William Carey campaigned to end the practice of widow-burning in India. Carey had not come to India to reform its social policies and change its culture. But as he preached the gospel, Carey saw numerous widows throw themselves on the funeral pyre of their husbands, killing themselves as an act of pagan worship. Over time, Carey sought to end this practice and succeeded. His coming to India meant the saving of many lives, as women experienced mercy instead of ritualistic death.

Fourth, the Exiles Blessed Babylon by a Stable Life

This tenet of *shalom*-seeking is admittedly implicit in Jeremiah 29. But it is not imaginary. God told the exiles to "seek the welfare of the city where I have sent you into exile," subtly reminding the remnant of Judah that he put them in Babylon. Their ZIP code was not a post office blunder. They lived in Babylon because God sent them there. Nor, as we saw above, had God commissioned them to take up arms against the pagan city. No, God called them to Babylon to become seven-decade citizens there.

God's people heard no call, then, to revolution. They were not to stockpile weapons in their gardens. They were not to plan a Midnight Takeover. They were not to assassinate government officials and destabilize the government. It is not a stretch to say that the example of Josiah riding out foolishly against Egypt was to instruct them. The remnant of Judah had arrived in Babylon in order to live there in unspectacular fashion. They were to accept Babylon, even, as J. A. Thompson points out:

> Jeremiah by these words cast the people completely adrift from all those things on which they depended and which they regarded as essential to their own well-being, a nation-state, kingship, an army, national borders, the temple. Without all these Yahweh could give the nation new perspectives and a new understanding of their calling.[9]

That was it; that was the grand plan. There was no exciting turnaround, no miracle rescue, no quick fix. There was a long line of faithfulness instead.

Along these lines, the Judahite exiles received the call from God to build. Instead of erecting temporary housing, God instructed them to build houses and live in them. This signified the stability of the exilic period. Instead of jumping around and practicing a liquid lifestyle, the remnant of Judah needed to settle in for the long haul. Their stability would, in fact, witness to their confidence in God and his plan (as we saw in Chapter 2).

The same is true for us today. We seek the *shalom* of our own location by embracing a "stable and steadfast" identity in Christ (see Colossians 1:23). On the basis of this identity, we choose stability in all of our lives. We build houses. If married, we build families. Whether single or married, we join and serve churches, strengthening the spiritual family of Christ as a member of it.

We do much the same in our community. As those who seek to lead a "quiet life" in dignity and peace (see 1 Timothy 2:2), we do all the little things that build stability. We strive to be a good neighbor. We take care of the home we build (or buy). We show kindness to those around us. We pray to make wise decisions that will pay off in the long term. In the area of finances, we do not shoot up and down like a Fourth of July firework, wildly speculating with our hard-earned money. We invest. We save. We practice frugality and godly stewardship.

As we embrace normality, we will likely feel the smallness of our efforts. But the strange truth is this: in our smallness there is greatness. A life built one decision at a time, one wise practice at a time, one act of forgiveness at a time, one choice to sacrifice our selfish interests at a time, one stable moment at a time is a well-built life.

Fifth, the Exiles Blessed Babylon by Prospering in It

God did not put the remnant of Judah in Babylon to sit by the pool, idling the hours away. God himself is a creator, a builder, and a worker. God is the original gardener, and he planted his people in Babylon not to crush it, but to cultivate it. So it was that God called his followers to prosper in a pagan place and bring greater flourishing not only for them but for the broader city.

One way we glorify God and serve others is by employing a *cultivation* mindset in our vocation. As we discussed in Chapter 3, God wanted his people to work, and work hard. Of course, we do not seek riches as the godless do. Money does not drive us. But Christians do recognize that God institutes, honors, and richly blesses hard work and market exchange.

We could put it this way: Scripture is no socialism textbook. Scripture teaches the goodness of labor, of building a vocation, of earning your keep, of saving and investing your money, and of seeing your God-given talents as a means of blessing others. As a community of Christians exhibits this ethic, such God-centered labor will bear witness. It will show unbelievers that there is another way to work besides self-centered striving or passive time-wasting. It is purposeful, joyful cultivation for the glory of God and the good of man.

As an example of this in history, we think of how biblical ideals influenced and ignited the Dutch. Holland is not a large country, but once the doctrines of the Reformation took hold, a zeal for free enterprise was unleashed. The Dutch became a prosperous people, and culture blossomed alongside the market, creating delicious food, beautiful homes, elegant culture, and a thriving civil order.

In recent years, young people have learned in many schools and universities that the "Protestant work ethic" is bad. In proper biblical balance, this simply is not true. Scriptural teaching about work has had marvelous effects when put into practice in different communities and countries. In many places, where the liberating gospel has gone, freedom has followed. We could put it this way:

- Gospel liberty (freed people) brings spiritual liberty (free churches).
- Spiritual liberty births religious liberty (freedom of conscience).
- Religious liberty undergirds political liberty (free citizens).
- Political liberty drives economic liberty (free markets).
- Economic liberty unleashes aesthetic liberty (free culture).

The free gospel creates free peoples, and free peoples create prosperity. This is not an iron law. However, as we have seen, God wants his people to thrive. He did not send the descendants of Judah into Babylon to die. He sent them into the great city to live in it, prosper in it, plant gardens in it, experience *shalom* in it, and bring that same *shalom* to others.

We do well to remember this in all facets of our lives, including our daily labor. Our prospering—as God leads and provides—is not an end unto itself. Our prospering glorifies God and reaches into the lives of others, enabling them to experience the good gifts of God as well. Abundance is not a hindrance to witness; abundance won through hard work *is* witness.

Sixth, the Exiles Blessed Babylon by Bringing Beauty to It

The text of Jeremiah 29 does not include explicit mention of beauty. I think, however, that there is a resonance in the text, for all that God calls for in the "plant gardens" passage shines with beauty. A garden, as we have discussed earlier, is in truth the original work of beauty, artwork in the natural realm. Houses, furthermore, can be beautiful; so too is the family itself a living garden, and thus beautiful. Beauty is interwoven throughout the "plant gardens" mandate to the exiles, I believe.

Beyond this section of Scripture, we believers do not struggle whatsoever to account for our thirst for beauty. We crave beauty because, as David captures in Psalm 27:4, our God is surpassingly beautiful: "One thing have I asked of the LORD, that will I seek after: that I may dwell in the house of the LORD all the days of my life, to gaze upon the beauty of the LORD and to inquire in his temple."

As Christians, we treasure beauty because our God is excellent. That is, he is both delightful to the senses and nourishing to the soul. He is what every person innately wants to find and yearns to gaze upon. He is true beauty itself. It is the over-spilling nature of his beauty, in fact, that compels us—his image-bearers—to create beauty in our own environment. As we have seen already in these pages, this can be a majestic art project, or it can be a flower in a $5 vase. Beauty does not have a price-tag; beauty is a way of life.

We find beauty all through it due to God's common grace. We celebrate what is excellent and skilled and lovely where we find it. Yes, sin corrupts all it touches; yes, depravity extends over all the face of the earth; yes, we must exercise watchfulness and discernment and much spiritual care in our fallen world. But nonetheless, we need not reject beauty. Instead, we should embrace it. We should create it. We should treasure it.

Again, this does not mean that we must all become a globally celebrated artist. Few of us can achieve such an outcome. I believe it means quite the opposite: that we democratize beauty, bringing it into our lives in all sorts of forms. We reject a utilitarian mindset in which we simply exist; we turn a cold shoulder to the machinization of our existence. We create things; we steward our homes and offices and land; we behold, listen to, and take in beauty wherever we can find it, whether this means we visit an art gallery or drive through a forest.

This is important material in the age of AI. You can write a computer code, I am guessing, to identify based on certain standards what is beautiful. But you cannot get that computer to *treasure* beauty. In similar fashion, you can have a program make you a movie, but you have no way to make that program *enjoy* the work of creation. This only a human can do. This only Christians will do with a God-centered focus.

Living in Babylon—then and now—does not mean giving up on beauty. It means the opposite. For one, where common grace had allowed the Babylonians to foster beauty, the people of God could appreciate it. So too with us. Everywhere we find beauty (of a moral kind), we can honor and enjoy it. But even more than this, the people of God were called to bring beauty into the everyday. To put it more simply, they were called to make their world beautiful. So are we.

Beauty, we remember, is a profound part of *shalom*. It is a pulsing element of the peace of God that contains every good thing and no bad thing. Just as the people of God beautified Babylon, so we can do the same.

Conclusion

It is remarkable how difficult it is for us fallen creatures to execute one simple task: do what we need to do. As I have experienced on occasion as a youth basketball coach, we excel in the opposite direction. We have a tendency to do anything but what we need to do. This is true of young men racing around a court; it is more broadly true of all of us. We speak when we should be quiet; we are quiet when we should speak. We act when we should slow down; we slow down when we should step up and act.

Our propensity to turn wisdom on its head syncs with what we see of God's people in Scripture. They are no different from us, and we are no better than them. At different times in Jeremiah's day, they *accommodated* pagan practices, adopting them with zeal. They *attacked* enemy nations, wrongly thinking that God had called them to conquest. They wanted to *abandon* their place of deportation, escaping the field of witness for the comfort of home.

Thankfully, our God is the God of second chances. Instead of accommodating, attacking, or abandoning our very own Babylon, we can hear Jeremiah 29:7 afresh and seek to aerate it. We can bring the *shalom* of the Word and gospel to it. Our calling is not to hate Babylon; our calling is to love Babylon, always standing on God's truth as we do so.

CHAPTER 6

Seek God

The Joy of Deep Spirituality

You will seek me and find me, when you seek me with all your heart.
—Jeremiah 29:13

Some years ago, scientist Richard Dawkins tendered this gentle opinion about God:

> The God of the Old Testament is arguably the most unpleasant character in all fiction: jealous and proud of it; a petty, unjust, unforgiving control-freak; a vindictive, bloodthirsty ethnic cleanser; a misogynistic, homophobic, racist, infanticidal, genocidal, filicidal, pestilential, megalomaniacal, sadomasochistic, capriciously malevolent bully.[1]

Dawkins published this broadside in 2006. He framed faith in God as nothing more than a "delusion," and many gravitated toward that conclusion. In fact, an entire intellectual movement coalesced around this contention: the New Atheism. Led by Dawkins, the controversial essayist Christopher Hitchens, the techbro Sam Harris, and the philosopher Daniel Dennett, the New Atheism grabbed headlines.

The New Atheists set the intellectual edge for years to come. They made atheism cool, and mocked Christianity mercilessly. In fact, they not only denigrated Christian faith, but made it the scapegoat for what ailed the world. As abuse scandals arose in the Catholic Church and Islam unleashed terror across the world, the New Atheists argued that religion—all religion—brought only wars and pain.

Where Dawkins threw down the gauntlet in the academy, Hitchens drew a line in the sand in the public square. Faith, he contended, is man's toddler-level attempt to understand the world:

> Religion comes from the period of human prehistory where nobody—not even the mighty Democritus who concluded that all matter was made from atoms—had the smallest idea what was going on. It comes from the bawling and fearful infancy of our species, and is a babyish attempt to meet our inescapable demand for knowledge (as well as for comfort, reassurance and other infantile needs).[2]

This scathing brand of commentary set the terms of conversation for years to come. Christianity was not to be engaged; Christianity, as with all religion, was to be mocked, rejected, and consigned to the dustbin of history. Many followed Dawkins and Hitchens in the early years of the twenty-first century, believing as they did so that they were entering a new era of mankind. In this time, religion would be displayed by reason, and the world would heal from its faith-caused wounds.

A World Unready for Pain

This is what many *thought* would happen. Indeed, for some time, Christianity did indeed go on the run in the West. (It still is in many ways.) Yet this retreat did not lead to the harvest season that the New Atheists and their publicists foretold. Instead, a remarkable coterie of bad ideas and evil ideologies arose. It was not so much one cultural thunderstorm as it was numerous storms colliding at once, threatening everything that many Westerners—Christians and skeptics alike—hold dear.

The catalogue of woe facing the West from roughly 2010 to 2022 boggles the mind. Pagan sexuality, wokeness, lockdowns, injurious medicine, strands of "MeToo," attacks on men, open borders, skyrocketing inflation, spiking suicide rates among teens, bad health in the era of processed food, boys in girls' restrooms—all this advanced rapidly at some time in this era, as we considered above in the Introduction.

For our purposes, here is what the entwined unleashing of these evils accomplished: it made the West unready for pain. It left people miserable. It rendered ordinary citizens targets of various nasty ideologies. If you had "white" skin, you were a "white supremacist." If you did not desire to have an experimental gene therapy injected into your body, you were a "vax denier." If you did not wish for your eight-year-old daughter to have a fifteen-year-old boy in her locker room, you were a "bigot."

Many people resigned themselves to this new normal. But in time, others started speaking up. Fascinatingly, some "freethinkers," agnostics, leftist comedians, and outright atheists became the fiercest critics of leftist views. Once they were its bravest cheerleaders; they morphed, however, into dogged skeptics.

They did so because they saw that something real and terrible was happening to their children and our civilization. Surrounded by anxiety, they realized that our world was unready for pain. So they spoke up. The foremost of these voices was Professor Jordan Peterson, but he was not alone. In the 2020s, politicians pushed back against leftist policies and won office. Health advocates questioned Big Food.

Injury sufferers raised their voice against mandated vaccinations that could cause terrible harm. Scientists challenged Big Pharma. Academics pushed back against wokeness. Men pushed back against "toxic masculinity." Citizens stood up to forced lockdowns. Parents spoke up against boys in girls' sports and spaces.

Fast forward to today. The pushback against wokeness, the "MeToo" movement, lockdowns, and leftist ideas generally has changed our culture. The failure of leftism to deliver stability and prosperity has left many people open once more to Christianity and its claims. More than has been true for decades, people today crave higher meaning and want deeper purpose.

Welcome to the Post "Post-Christian" Age

In recent days in the West, something remarkable has happened: among the rising generation, interest in Christianity is rising, even as profession of atheism is waning. We have arrived—all of a sudden, like a plane making an unplanned landing—in the post "post-Christian" age. Author and podcaster Justin Brierley was early to this trend, and in 2023, offered this astute observation:

> Most significantly, as the influence of New Atheism has waned, a variety of secular thinkers have been stepping forward to ask new questions about the value of religion and where the West is heading in the absence of the Christian story. . . . Many even seem to harbor a wistful desire for Christianity to be true. As their influence has grown, it has led me to wonder whether, even in the midst of our highly secular culture, we are witnessing a sea change in people's openness to faith.[3]

Recent events have only confirmed Brierley's anecdotal insight. Jordan Peterson has written major works and produced a hugely popular video series on the Bible. Ayaan Hirsi Ali, a one-time New Atheism superstar, has professed Christian faith. Here is what Ali wrote about her formerly atheistic life:

> Yet I would not be truthful if I attributed my embrace of Christianity solely to the realisation that atheism is too weak and divisive a doctrine to fortify us against our menacing foes. I have also turned to Christianity because I ultimately found life without any spiritual solace unendurable—indeed very nearly self-destructive. Atheism failed to answer a simple question: what is the meaning and purpose of life?[4]

Ali's husband, the eminent historian Niall Ferguson, has offered similar testimony. In an interview with Canada's Macdonald-Laurier Institute, Ferguson renounced his former skeptical ways and said this about his newfound faith: "I found in the end that atheism was not a basis for a meaningful life—and certainly not for a happy family life. And so I and my wife recently were baptized, and are now practicing and devout Christians, and it has made a profound change to my life."[5]

In sports, numerous athletes have professed faith in Christ, as seen when many members of the Ohio State football team wore—at the start of their 2024–25 season—"Jesus Won" t-shirts. So too in pop culture. In music, Forrest Frank is as popular a rising artist as one can find; his blend of sunny California pop-rap is ubiquitous. On YouTube Music, for example, Frank recently drew more monthly listeners than the rapper Drake, a stunning achievement.[6]

So too with Christian music. One site reported that in 2025, "Christian music is surging in mainstream popularity, with 60% growth in Spotify streams globally over five years."[7] A report from NPR found the same trend in culture: "This year, Marconette says christian/gospel music overall has overtaken world music, a genre that encompasses K-pop and Afrobeats. 'We've never seen that before,' he says." According to the article, while predominantly older audiences formerly gravitated to CCM, a younger demographic now makes up 45 percent of the overall CCM audience, with no signs of decreasing.[8]

As in music, so in book sales. Following the martyrdom of Charlie Kirk in September 2025, Bible sales rocketed in America.

According to the *Wall Street Journal*, "There were 2.4 million Bibles sold in the U.S. in September, a 36% jump over the same month of 2024, according to book tracker Circana BookScan."[9] Despite a slight dip in print book sales overall in America, Bible sales were up 11 percent in the year as a whole, a notable increase.

So too have Bible sales soared overseas. In January 2026, the *Daily Mail* reported a remarkable upsurge in purchasing compared to pre-COVID sales:

> Bible sales in Britain have hit their highest level on record after more than doubling compared to pre-pandemic levels, driven by a surge in interest from Gen Z. Total UK sales of the religious text reached £6.3million last year—up 134 per cent in value since £2.7million in 2019, according to analysis of Nielsen BookScan data. Sales have also risen by 106 per cent in volume over the same period. Between 2024 and 2025, sales went up by 25 per cent in value and 28 per cent in volume.[10]

A "Quiet Revival" in Britain

The same trends applied—perhaps most shockingly of all—to church attendance. Church growth professionals have fostered a cottage industry in the West with their measures to attract youth to worship services. Against all the odds, and with little improvement in marketing and aesthetics, young people are doing something truly countercultural: they are going to church. This is true not only in America, but in the famously "post-Christian" United Kingdom.

No less a cultural authority than *The Times of London* devoted major attention to this development, pointing to data showing that church attendance has quadrupled among young adults. The outlet went so far as to call this a "quiet revival":

> These are two sides of the much-discussed "quiet revival" in Christian faith among young people. "Global crises sending Gen Z to church" bawled a Sunday Express front page a couple of weeks ago. The empirical foundation of the chatter is a study commissioned by the Bible Society earlier this year which found a quadrupling of church attendance among young adults, from 4 per cent in 2018 to 16 per cent now.[11]

In a different piece, *The Times of London* reported that eighteen to twenty-four-year-olds ranked as far more "spiritual" than other demographics. "Asked if they have a spiritual side, 62 per cent of 18 to 24-year-olds said they are 'very' or 'fairly' spiritual, compared to just 35 per cent of those aged over 65, 36 per cent of those aged 55 to 64, and 52 per cent of those aged 35 to 44."[12]

As I noted above, Christianity is on the rise among the young. Atheism, by contrast, is declining in popularity. According to *The Times of London*, "The least likely group to call themselves atheists, however, are those aged under 25, only 13 per cent of whom identify as such." As in the UK, so in America. The Barna Group offered a striking assessment in early September 2025: "Millennials and Gen Z are driving a resurgence in church attendance."[13]

The research done by Barna disclosed the remarkable fact that

> Millennials and Gen Z Christians are attending church more frequently than before and much more often than are older generations. The typical Gen Z churchgoer now attends 1.9 weekends per month, while Millennial churchgoers average 1.8 times—a steady upward shift since the lows seen during the pandemic.

We cannot underplay how significant these findings are. Against all the groundwork laid by the leading lights of leftism, young people have turned away from secularism. They are buying Bibles. They are listening to Christian music. They are going to church. They are identifying as spiritual, not atheist. They are open to spirituality, to transcendence, and to greater meaning once more.

The Bright Hope of a Believing Future

What a welcome development this is. Once again, people all around us are taking their spiritual lives seriously. Many who have been told that we are only matter and have no higher purpose are finding this an extremely inhospitable—and even downright miserable—worldview. In a hard time in the West, people are finding that the pleasing fictions they were once sold offer no solace and no comfort.

This hot new trend is actually a historic one. The exiles of Judah made just such a discovery as they began a new season in Babylon. Though they faced a real trial in the form of their deportation, God was there for them. God, furthermore, had a mission for them, a call to cultivate. But this was not all. Following Jeremiah

29:4–7, God laid out a bright future for the people of God in Jeremiah 29:10–14, which we turn to now:

> For thus says the LORD: When seventy years are completed for Babylon, I will visit you, and I will fulfill to you my promise and bring you back to this place. For I know the plans I have for you, declares the LORD, plans for welfare and not for evil, to give you a future and a hope. Then you will call upon me and come and pray to me, and I will hear you. You will seek me and find me, when you seek me with all your heart. I will be found by you, declares the LORD, and I will restore your fortunes and gather you from all the nations and all the places where I have driven you, declares the LORD, and I will bring you back to the place from which I sent you into exile.

Even as the exiles faced challenging days in Babylon for the next seven decades, God offered them profound hope. This hope centered not so much in external blessings, although those would come. This hope centered squarely in *relational communion.* This is what God made humanity for; this is what redeemed humanity gets to experience. It is this fellowship, this loving knowledge of the living God, that every human person seeks, and that the followers of Christ taste in full.

I cannot stress this enough. The chief good of following God is God himself. Nothing is better than knowing God. Knowing God is truly the end, the crowning purpose, of the Christian faith. It is what the human person was made for, and it is how we find meaning, purpose, hope, joy, fulfillment, and pleasure in a fallen world. Knowing God is not simply the *gateway* to the good life; knowing God *is* the good life.

This is what Jeremiah articulated to the exiles in Babylon. Speaking God's own words, Jeremiah called the people to see that God still wanted relational communion with them. Though the people had wandered from God, and though God had acted to judge their sins in righteousness, yet he desired warm fellowship with them once more. The people had chosen brokenness and pain over closeness with God, but God had not abandoned them. This is because God—as we have seen—is a relational God.

The character of the biblical God is wondrous beyond words. Over against some common conceptions of the divine, the biblical God is not a distant God. The biblical God is transcendent, perfect in holiness, yet loves to draw near to his creation (Acts 17:27). The biblical God is not impersonal; the biblical God is vibrantly personal, a reality that begins in Trinitarian love and spills over into the life of his redeemed people.

This God is not disinterested in the world he made, having stepped away from it after creating it. The biblical God has chosen to invest his glory in this place, giving great energy and attention to the formation of a people for himself. The biblical God is not uncaring; the biblical God cares in the most attentive and tender way for his people, always seeking their good (see 1 Peter 5:7).

The God Who Loves to Love

It is this loving God who calls to his people in verses 10–14. There are three key elements to the relational communion between

Yahweh and his covenant people as recorded by Jeremiah. We will look briefly at them now.

First, Relational Communion Flows from God's Truth (vv. 10–11)

Our intimate knowledge of God obviously engages our entire emotional makeup. But at base, knowing God happens when we learn about God in his Word. Our relationship is based entirely on God's truth and God's revelation, not our feelings. In the context of our passage, the Judahites were not going to be blessed because they wanted to be blessed or had strong desires to be blessed. The Judahites would be blessed in days ahead because God had amazing "plans" for them, plans "to give you a future and a hope" (v. 11).

Relational communion only happens when we know God as he has revealed himself. In our walk of faith, we are not creating God in our image, then; we are receiving God as he desires to be known. He sets the terms. He structures the relationship. He calls the shots. He is the Creator; we are the creature. He is the Sustainer; we are the ones needing to be sustained.

The wonderful truth, though, is that he does not wield his power wickedly against us, but rather marshals all the resources of his divine sovereignty and wisdom to bless those who have wandered from him. This was true in Babylon, and it is equally true today. God had a specific plan for the exiles, but God is working out the same plan in our time that he was in the sixth century BC. This plan centers in the saving and blessing of the people chosen by God for his glory (see Ephesians 1:3–14).

Second, Relational Communion Involves Calling on God and Praying to Him (v. 12)

When the seventy years of exile in Babylon concluded, then God promised that his people would call upon him. At that time, he would hear them. It was a long education in dependence that God enrolled the people of Judah in, but this lengthy period of training would bear great fruit. Specifically, it would show the exiles how greatly they needed God, a discovery all humanity needs to make.

The language God used was of drawing near in physical terms: "Then you will call upon me and come and pray to me, and I will hear you." This language has spiritual meaning, signaling that instead of hanging back, the exiles would again approach God. They would not run from him; they would not try to leave his presence. They would, in great need, draw near to him. The form this spiritual nearness took would be prayer. Here is the very currency of relational communion: dependent and humble prayer to God. This is what the people would offer to their sovereign.

For his part, God promised to "hear" them. No relationship can be strong without both sides hearing the other and listening well to one another. The biblical God reveals himself, strikingly, as a God who *wants* to hear from his people. He wants them—and us—to pray. He does not desire that we keep our troubles to ourselves and figure things out on our own. God wants our trust, our expressed need, our humble requests. All this takes shape in and is expressed by prayer.

Third, Relational Communion Means Seeking God with All Our Heart (vv. 13–14)

We cannot say it too strongly: the biblical God *loves* relationship. As stated above, he is anything but impersonal. He is nothing if not communicative. He has infinite satisfaction in himself, yet he wanted to create a world with tiny bearers of his image in it and know them in the deepest possible way. This is where God's plans eventually led for the exiles: they would "seek" him (v. 13). But not only this: they would surely "find" him.

The biblical God is the God who wants to be found. When the people would return to him, he promised to bless them beyond all imagining. He would grant them back their "fortunes" and resettle them in Jerusalem, "the place from which I sent you into exile" (v. 14). The lesson here for us is this: when we pursue God with all our heart, mind, soul, and strength, he generously rewards such grace-driven effort. He in no way holds back his blessing from us.

To the contrary, as God's people seek him, he makes himself eminently findable. As we return to him, he gives us the greatest gift we can fathom: the gift of warm, tender, intimate, and deeply loving communion. God is the reward of those who desire his blessings. God is the greatest blessing that God can give. To know God is to not only possess the pearl of great price spoken of by Christ, but to treasure and enjoy that pearl every second one has it (see Matthew 13:45–46).

Of course, God loves to give many other good gifts as well. God is a cheerful and generous giver, and there is no limit to his gift-giving inclination. We need never fear—as Christians often do—that once God has given us a gift, he has exhausted his kindness to us. Scripture sounds the opposite note, as Paul states in uplifting terms: "And God is able to make all grace abound to you, so that having all sufficiency in all things at all times, you may abound in every good work" (2 Corinthians 9:8).

This weight of glorious doctrine points us squarely in one direction: toward God. We need to seek God with our whole heart. But we do not do so as Christians from a posture of terror, nor of rote moralistic duty. We seek God because God loves to be known, and God pours love through us as we draw near to him. The God we love is the God who loves to love.

Drawing Near to God

God's promise of blessing to his people in Jeremiah 29:10–14 reminds us that God loves his people in all seasons. He gives us hope, future hope, even as he stays close by us at all times. We need to remember his steadfastness if we are to have a thriving walk with God. God is with us. God has good for us. God is not about to cancel his promises for the age to come; God is accomplishing everything that he said he would do. God is helping us, equipping us, and strengthening us in all our ups and downs.

When we know that God is near to us, we are freed to reciprocate. The New Testament has a simple phrase for such a relationship: as God draws near to us, so we can draw near to God (see James 4:8). Instead of hanging back and staying away from God, we press in to know him. We take our soul seriously. Confident in his love, we study God in order to commune with God.

There is a wondrous warmness in this truth. It frees us to see that the sovereign God is not a remote God. The sovereign God wants to be known. He has made it not only possible for us to know him; he has drawn near to us and given us certain disciplines by which we can experience the warmth of his presence.

God is not hard to find, then. Nor is relational communion with him a complex enterprise. As we have seen already, God is marvelously near to all who will call on him in humble faith. To become a Christian and cultivate a spiritual walk, then, is not hard; it is simple, gloriously simple.

How Can We Cultivate Our Spiritual Walk?

We have made the case that Christianity is meant to be lived, not merely debated in the court of public opinion. The question before us, then, in the closing section of this chapter is this: How do we live in relational communion with the living God? Or, said differently, what does it look like to become a man or woman of God who communes with the Lord on a regular basis? In what follows, here are five key practices of a thriving faith that lead to greater spiritual closeness with God.

First, Cultivate a Relationship with God

Many people are searching. They are interested in "spirituality." When I hear of someone who has opened themselves up to genuine spiritual inquiry, I am glad. In Scripture, it is indeed right to recognize the existence of the soul and the need for God. But the entire New Testament teaches that we do not freelance from this point forward, following whatever inclinations or desires we have in a spiritual direction. To know God, we must know the one who imaged God on earth, Jesus Christ.

Put another way: the only way to true spirituality is through the gospel. Jesus Christ alone is "the way, the truth, and the life" (John 14:6). There are not many paths to God; there is one path to God. This means that we can indeed have a relationship with God, we can commune with God deeply, but we cannot do so any which way we see fit. We must know the gospel, repent of our sins, and trust Christ as our Savior to have a relationship with God.

Faith and repentance in the name of Christ is the first step in knowing God. From there, a lifetime of knowing and being known by the divine ensues. This is a beautiful, exhilarating, challenging, and eternally rewarding pursuit. Everything hangs upon it, in truth. Without such a relationship, we will suffer the eternal judgment of God in hell. But with Christ as our Savior, we can know for absolute certain that we will live forever with God in a world of love.

Second, Cultivate Communion with God Through Study

Our culture divorces the heart from the mind. This is an extremely unhelpful way to live, for God designed our mind and heart to work together. But for believers in Christ, the knowledge of God is not a merely intellectual pursuit. In striving to know God through the study of Scripture, we are not simply storing up facts. Through study of God's truth, God affects not only our mind, but our entire being, renewing us in a comprehensive way.

Paul gives us just this vision of godly knowledge in Romans 12:2. "Do not be conformed to this world," he urges, "but be transformed by the renewal of your mind, that by testing you may discern what is the will of God, what is good and acceptable and perfect." As sinners, here is the cold truth: we *are* conformed to the world. Thoroughly. Across the board. When God saves us, he initiates a lifelong process of transformation. Our transformation comes from "the renewal" of our "mind." We stop following lies, and we start following truth.

We study Scripture, cultivating what we call a "devotional walk." We strive to make Bible reading a habit, but more than a habit, a *reflex*. Bible reading is not a box we check to feel good about our pious behavior; Bible reading is delicious food for a starving soul. As we feed on all the truth of God, something wonderful plays out: we gradually "discern" the "will of God," figuring out "what is good and acceptable and perfect."

In a subtle way, this passage reframes our understanding of divine guidance. The Word is chock-full of wisdom. The Spirit is a guiding Spirit. In normal terms, God does not intervene in spectacular ways to direct us. God calls us to take in Scripture, pray over everything before us, and then God leads us in a "testing" pattern. To put it differently, God moves us to think, to pray, to process, to weigh our decisions according to Scripture, to get counsel, and then to act in faith.

As we study God to know God, we will gain an ever-strengthening love for God. The transformation of our mind will foster the transformation of our affections. The more we know God, the more we will love God. This will in turn deepen our relationship with God. We will wake up to the very purpose for which we were made: to enjoy delicious communion with our Creator, Redeemer, and Lord.

We cannot sum up the point better than J. I. Packer:

> [T]hough God is a great King, it is not his wish to live at a distance from his subjects. Rather the reverse: he made us with the intention that he and we might walk together forever in a love relationship. But such a relationship can exist only when the parties involved know something of each other. God, our Maker, knows all about us before we say anything (Ps. 139:1–4); but we can know nothing about him unless he tells us. Here, therefore, is a further reason why God speaks to us: not only to move us to do what he wants, but to enable us to know him so that we may love him.[14]

Third, Cultivate Communion with God Through Prayer

In knowing God through a living relationship, we gain "pleasures forevermore" (Psalm 16:11). This has immediate cash value for our practical faith. In the simplest terms, but also the most profound terms, we should make the primary business of our lives to savor communion with God. This means that we develop a strong prayer life. We go to God in prayer frequently through the day. We get off our screens, stow away our phones, and get out into nature.

In terms resonant with the call to prayer in Jeremiah 29:7, we should pray for unbelievers. We should ask God to show mercy to many around us, remembering that we ourselves are no better than they. If God can save a sinner like us, he can save them. We should ask God to save our children and family members. We should pray for God to work in the hearts and minds of rulers and authorities, both redemptively and for the good of society.

What Jeremiah 29 announced as a shift, Jesus brought to fulfillment. We should not just generically pray for lost people; Jesus went so far as to teach his disciples to pray for their enemies.

> You have heard that it was said, "You shall love your neighbor and hate your enemy." But I say to you, Love your enemies and pray for those who persecute you, so that you may be sons of your Father who is in heaven. For he makes his sun rise on the evil and on the good, and sends rain on the just and on the unjust. (Matthew 5:43–45)

This is a richly inspiring call to prayer. It upends every natural human expectation we have. As addressed in the opening part of this chapter, this call to prayer from Jesus brings to fruition the divine instruction from Jeremiah. Disciples of Jesus do not only dwell in fallen locations, we see here; our charge from God goes much further, necessitating a prayer life for those who most dislike us, oppose us, and even persecute us (see Jeremiah 29:44).[15]

The gospel of grace transforms our natural instincts. It drives us to pray and helps us grasp the true nature of prayer. Though prayer feels small and quiet, Scripture teaches us that it is actually quite powerful. James says this directly: "The prayer of a righteous person has great power as it is working" (James 5:16). Prayer, in truth, *is* resistance—resistance against doubt, against fear, against the ever-expanding cluster of anxiety at our core. Prayer is powerful.

Fourth, Cultivate Your Church as a Servant

Aside from your personal walk with God, very close to the most important element of your entire life is this: being a member of a sound church. More than you know, you need to be under a team of godly and gracious shepherds who can feed your soul, care for your soul, watch over your soul, and lead you spiritually.

For this reason, the church you join ranks as nearly the most important decision you will make. There is no perfect congregation, of course. Every flock has its weaknesses, failings, and shortcomings. However, there are some strong churches out there, and I encourage you to do what you can to find one. In terms that mirror your care for your body, if you "eat" a healthy spiritual diet from skilled chefs (pastors), you will—by and large—grow healthy.

So, here is a friendly encouragement: find, join, and serve a healthy church. I am referring to a church that features faithful and honest preaching of the Word of God. Gracious proclamation of the gospel. Loving member care by elders who actually enjoy shepherding the flock (and do not see this as a burden or a rote duty). A healthy body life that activates the gifts of the membership, offers opportunities for service and evangelism, and warmly unites people in the name of Christ.

A key part of maturing is stepping off of the sidelines. God has not saved you to be a passive consumer. God has saved you to be a servant-hearted cultivator. We hear just such a description of true

Christianity in Matthew 20:26b–27 from the mouth of Jesus: "But whoever would be great among you must be your servant, and whoever would be first among you must be your slave." In the kingdom of Christ, greatness is not self-exaltation. Greatness is self-sacrifice. In a word, service.

On this count, I recall the powerful testimony of a former English lawyer named Stephen Foster.[16] While a lawyer (or "barrister," as the British call it), Foster was asked to serve on the "coffee team." In a video, Foster shared how this simple request first bothered him, but then changed him:

> I was at the back of our church in East London and someone said to me, "We need help to run the coffee team." And I was like working 70, 80 hours a week and I'm like, "What?" And they're like, "Yeah, Steve, we need your help running the coffee team on a Sunday."

At this point, Foster thought this: "I've got a job. I don't need another job." The call to servanthood initially rubbed him the wrong way, and he thought of the small act of service as meaningless. But when he begrudgingly decided to serve one week, something awoke in him:

> As I handed these cups to people, something really changed in me. I found myself, as I handed coffee to these people, growing in love for them. I thought, "These people are amazing. This is this extraordinarily diverse community that's been gathered from across the area.

> There's probably not another place that looks as diverse and integrated as this. This is a miracle."

The church wasn't perfect, Foster knew. But by his own declaration, Foster saw something happen in him: "I kind of basically fell in love with the church." He then became a dynamo of coffee, seeking to improve the coffee ministry, wanting to give people the best product they could get: "We need new coffee machines. We need better beans. We need better mugs. Come on, these are amazing people! I want this to be the best coffee that they get."

This testimony went viral a few years ago, and for good reason. It elegantly encapsulates the servant mentality that rests at the center of the Christian faith. We are not here to use our gifts on ourselves. God made us to use our gifts for his glory and others' good. Alongside our family and our vocation, the local church serves as the primary spiritual outlet of this activity. We will flourish when we cultivate our church, which is to say, when we serve it.

Fifth, Cultivate Deep Roots to Withstand Trials

We have squared with reality in the pages of this book. We have straightforwardly observed that it is no easy thing to live in Babylon. Navigating a fallen world means depending on God, walking by faith, and enduring much hardship. This last element is not the part of true spirituality that many want to consider. In fact, many people embrace "spirituality" of some kind in order to get out of hardship. They think that if they just tune in to their spiritual side, their problems will disappear.

Nothing could be further from the truth. Jesus, we recall, told us—via his disciples—to expect tribulation and suffering on this earth (see John 16:33). This is a major reason why we need to cultivate our faith. We are all going to face trials, even severe ones, and we need deep roots if we are going to make it through them. Failure to get ready for this reality will not help us or our loved ones; failure to prepare for winter means we only bring on more pain and suffering that we could ever have imagined.

So it is that we cultivate our walk with Christ. We get ready for Babylon, even as we get others ready for Babylon. Our mentality matters greatly here. True spirituality does not pretend suffering does not exist; true spirituality grapples with the harshness of our suffering, viewing it in a God-centered perspective, as Paul does in 2 Corinthians 4:7–12.

> But we have this treasure in jars of clay, to show that the surpassing power belongs to God and not to us. We are afflicted in every way, but not crushed; perplexed, but not driven to despair; persecuted, but not forsaken; struck down, but not destroyed; always carrying in the body the death of Jesus, so that the life of Jesus also may be manifested in our bodies. For we who live are always being given over to death for Jesus' sake, so that the life of Jesus also may be manifested in our mortal flesh. So death is at work in us, but life in you.

Over against a happy-clappy Christianity, one in which we pretend that pain is nonexistent and our lives are spotless, Paul invites us into an honest faith. He encourages us to practice truthfulness about darkness. His approach displays remarkable balance. He is ruggedly honest about how hard his missionary journeys have been, as he describes himself as "afflicted in every way," "perplexed," "persecuted," "struck down," and always living in proximity to "the death of Jesus." His ministry knows many downs, in other words.

While Paul is honest about his hardships, he emphasizes God's goodness. Through Paul's pain, God works "life in you," the embattled Corinthian church (v. 12). In even more piercing language, Paul expounds upon the good effect of his personal suffering in the cause of Christ:

> So we do not lose heart. Though our outer self is wasting away, our inner self is being renewed day by day. For this light momentary affliction is preparing for us an eternal weight of glory beyond all comparison, as we look not to the things that are seen but to the things that are unseen. For the things that are seen are transient, but the things that are unseen are eternal. (2 Corinthians 4:16–18)

Paul is tempted, we note, to "lose heart." In fact, at one particularly searing moment of ministry, he "despaired of life itself" (2 Corinthians 1:8). Yet by the grace of God, he did not lose it all. He had an "eternal perspective," as Christians have called it. He saw that God was doing a bigger work for his glory amidst all the pain of his people. This broader truth reframed suffering, causing Paul to label it a "light momentary affliction" (v. 17). Paul's pain paled in comparison to the "eternal weight of glory" that awaits every Christian.

In our spiritual lives, we must cultivate this same eternal perspective. We need not pretend that our own suffering is imaginary. It is not. It is all too real, and it can leave a serious mark on us, affecting us for many months, years, and even decades. But our suffering is not greater than God, and our pain is not more powerful than grace. God grows us not by taking away affliction, we remember, but by growing us as we experience it.

A Time of Awakening?

We began this chapter by hearing from Richard Dawkins. If you recall, he made the argument that the Old Testament was, essentially, horrible. Nothing good came from following such a "pestilential" and "sadomasochistic" figure, Dawkins avowed. These were shocking words in their day, and they continue to ripple across the waves of popular discourse, nearly two decades later.

But Dawkins had another surprise to give the world. In March 2024 during an interview with Leading Britain's Conversation, Dawkins announced to the world that he is a "cultural Christian."[17] Speaking with Leading Britain's Conversation, Dawkins said the following:

> I'm not a believer, but there is a distinction between being a believing Christian and a cultural Christian. I love hymns and Christmas carols and I sort of feel at home in the Christian ethos, and I feel that we are a Christian country in that sense.[18]

The Christian faith does not reduce only to "Christmas carols," of course. But it does bring delight, and that delight lasts long after Christmas season concludes. Indeed, the joy that spills out in the Christmas and Easter seasons is none other than the joy that believers possess at all times in Christ. The God who has made himself known desires *relational communion* with a redeemed people.

I thought of Dawkins's shocking admission following the tragic death of Charlie Kirk, the conservative activist slain in Utah in September 2025. Something strange and unusual played out after Kirk died; in truth, Kirk's martyrdom fanned into flame a movement among the rising generation that had already been growing in the months and years prior. This movement was driven by numerous people, but Kirk was undoubtedly a key voice within it.

We have seen data in this very chapter that shows—unequivocally—a spiritual awakening of sorts in the West. But when I went to Kirk's memorial service at the Cardinals Stadium in Glendale, Arizona, on September 21, 2025, I saw firsthand evidence of it that reaches far deeper than polling. For one, the crowd at Kirk's service was unlike anything I have ever seen. Though the crowds were massive, the general tone was not angry.

A spiritual seriousness hung in the air as worship music wafted through the building, creating a calming environment despite the grief we felt. During one song called "Gratitude," the entire arena quieted. The singer began the first line of the stanza, but then backed away as the crowd sang along. All around me, people lifted up their hands in worship. To a degree I've never seen in a public event in America, tears streamed down peoples' faces. In that arena, it was as if the pain and confusion and sorrow and anxiety we had felt since word first spread on social media of Kirk being shot was being washed away.

As I stood in that stadium, surrounded by strangers who seemed bonded in this transcendent moment, it felt like the first moment of healing since Charlie was slain in public. We were not healing because we raged. Nor because we chanted angry slogans. Nor because we protested anyone at that time. We were healing, our burdens silently lifted by the unseen hand of God, because we were lifting up our eyes to our Creator.

We were not looking down at our phones in that moment; we were not scheming or politicking or strategizing. We were doing something far more important, far more radical, and far more consequential: we were worshiping God. It was a unique and special moment. In that stadium, I saw grown men, many of them young, with tears running down their cheeks. I saw young women praising God in a terrible time.

For a brief and shining moment, I witnessed a generation come to life. After years of terrible political developments, national instability, mental health battles, and spiritual decline, I saw young men and women doing what is most needful, and most powerful, in this world: looking to God.

Conclusion

We have much more data to collect about our current spiritual moment. Only time will tell what exactly is playing out in the West. However, even as we prayerfully wait on God in this momentous time, we remember that our God is the God who specializes in redemption. This God can turn whole cultures around. He can stop the advance of the New Atheism led by men like Dawkins, and he can reach young men and women through the campus evangelism of Charlie Kirk.

Our world is rough and has gotten rougher, filling many with anxiety and sadness. But there is hope, divine hope. Just as God was able to revive his flagging people in Babylon, so he is able to do the same in ours. Who knows what God will do in days ahead? I for one am no prophet. However, my Bible teaches me one promise for certain: if we will draw near to God, Scripture promises, God will draw near to us (see James 4:8).

May it be so for us, and for many who now wander in the far country.

CHAPTER 7

National Cultivation

Christian Witness in a Secular Realm

Therefore render to Caesar the things that are Caesar's, and to God the things that are God's.
—Matthew 22:21

Politics is making you anxious.

It is for most of us, anyway. In 2024, for example, one study showed that about 80 percent of people felt anxiety over the presidential election.[1] This is true for the political junkies, sure, but it was also true of those who simply stay up to speed on politics. In an age of hyper-connectivity, social media cat-fights, and a never-ending news cycle, politics are a major part of our lives.

To put it mildly, this reality does not tend to induce peace and calmness. On all sides of the spectrum, many people today feel perpetual low-level worry about our country. The sky is always falling. The world is always just about to fall apart. A new national crisis arises by the week. Fights and political violence break out regularly. Small wonder that many Americans, and many Christians, live in a state of unrelieved anxiety over our nation.

Political Paranoia

In truth, this is not a new phenomenon. Over sixty years ago, the historian Richard Hofstadter called attention to the "paranoid style" of American politics. Given the turbulent founding of America and the civilizational disruptions this country has known over the years, Americans tend to play political hardball in an all-or-nothing mindset.

Describing the typical "paranoid spokesman," Hofstadter argued that this figure "sees the fate of this conspiracy in apocalyptic terms—he traffics in the birth and death of whole worlds, whole political orders, whole systems of human values."[2] This kind of leader is "militant" and uncompromising. He offers people wholesale good depicted against the backdrop of wholesale evil:

> Since the enemy is thought of as being totally evil and totally unappeasable, he must be totally eliminated—if not from the world, at least from the theatre of operations to which the paranoid directs his attention. This demand for total triumph leads to the formulation of hopelessly unrealistic goals, and since these goals are not even remotely attainable, failure constantly heightens the paranoid's sense of frustration.[3]

Hofstadter had his own biases, to be sure. But he put his finger on something real in the American tradition. In this country, politics tends to be treated as a gladiatorial contest, a fight to the death. Americans of all sides seem susceptible to the idea that the fate of the country hangs in the balance in every election, an approach grounded in anxiety that produces still more anxiety.

I myself believe that we should engage politics. However, I also need to acknowledge the clear and present danger of doing so: we may well be tempted to view politics as the vehicle by which the world will be made right. In such a state of mind, it is not hard for people of all persuasions—including Christians—to form "hopelessly unrealistic goals" and for politics to become a kind of wish-fulfillment exercise, in which only the biggest possible goal seems achievable.

The Rise of Christian Nationalism

In recent years, I believe that some Christians have been led to put their hope in political transformation. Just a few years ago, "Christian Nationalism" emerged as a cause starting in roughly 2022–23 (henceforth "CN"). CN came to the fore in a time when many believers—myself included—battled deep discouragement over the state of America.[4]

Seeing major problems in American public life, a movement, inchoate but energetic, arose. Under the banner of CN, it promised to sweep evil away and "Christianize" America. While "Christian Nationalism" has famously eluded careful definition, here are some of its core ideas:

- Nations can either be Christian or not.
- America was founded as a Christian nation.
- Secularism has taken America into the depths.

- So too has the political right embraced a "postwar consensus" ordered around "neutrality" that has robbed America of its spiritual character.
- American identity as Christian was grounded in actual people, many of whom shared Protestant convictions, European heritage, and "white" skin.
- Today, we need to reclaim this Anglo-Saxon identity and normalize it as the basis of our nation (this is often called "ethnonationalism").
- We also need to move away from the US Constitution (for it was made only for a moral people, which we are not), even as we need to reject "religious liberty" (which is tolerance of wicked unbelief) and embrace patriarchy (with home-owning men alone voting in elections), punishment of idolatry, enforcement of spiritual practice, and the adoption of Old Covenant law.[5]

A Radical Call: To Christianize the World

In CN, secularism looms large. The world is an all-or-nothing battlefront, with everything framed in black and white. It is either "Christ or Chaos." Neutrality is a fiction. When driven by a "post-millennial" outlook, this means that the call of the church is to take over every institution, every office, every community, and every state for Christ.

This has particular relevance for politics. The CN project invests great significance in formal Christianity at various levels. It is ideal and only right for America to be Christian, the argument goes. As boldly as this is proclaimed, though, it is rarely so boldly defined. For America to be Christian seems to mean—for many CN advocates—that the country is formally declared to be Christian, that Christian faith is privileged in law and policy, and that Christian laws are enacted.

This last tenet is of major importance for understanding Christian Nationalism. For most advocates of CN, the focus is on making and enforcing Christian laws. Preaching drives this political action, but political action is at the burning center of CN. In fact, CN is basically a political cure to what ails us. Surrounded by sin, CN leaders direct our attention to politics. If we are going to arrest our civilization's decline, we must embrace a radical approach to politics; we must "Christianize" the nation, or else we will lose it.

Christian Nationalism offers a cure for our political anxiety: a political Christianity. This vision has some strengths. It rightly takes Christ's Lordship seriously. It refuses to take evil lying down. Instead of quieting the Christian faith, it seeks to unleash Christian commitment on the world. CN advocates have boldly stood up against numerous societal evils, choosing to stand against public sin directly. They understand that the Christian faith is a forward-moving faith, and that believers need a driving purpose to thrive.

But while CN has some strengths, it also has some weaknesses. For starters, CN is not conservatism. CN is radicalism. It calls for a demolition of the existing political order of America. It argues that the Constitution no longer works for the American populace, and that we need the institution of Old Testament law to save our country.

Beyond this, CN addresses anxiety over politics by offering a political cure. All too often, the focus of CN is not *Christ*; the focus of CN is *Christianization*. Instead of lifting our eyes up to God, CN directs our hope to worldly efforts. We need not wait on Jesus to heal the world; we ourselves can heal the world, and in fact, we must do this. Anyone who fails to join us in this mission is failing the cause of Christianization.

As I have said, it makes sense why this outlook would appeal to some believers. Many of us are anxious about politics. We want things to be *fixed*. We want to see the world made right. We are tired of fallenness, and we yearn for strong leaders who will come along and build something good. Anxious people, furthermore, can become frustrated with God-based solutions. We want to *get things done*. We are tired of waiting. We are sick of fallenness.

Frustrated with our surroundings, we convince ourselves that it is in our power to change our context. This mindset may seem deeply optimistic, but in truth, it is fiercely anxious. In similar terms, it is not centered in God; it may begin with God, but it ends up being centered on us.

The Promise of a New and Better Covenant

As we have observed in this book, the temptation to ground our hope in ourselves and our nation is not new. We saw in Chapter 5 that the exiles to Babylon tried everything they could in earthly terms to get out of their own civilizational crisis. They accommodated Babylon; they fought back against it; they tried to leave it forever. They applied every worldly curative they could imagine to their troubles. None of these efforts worked; all of them, in fact, made things much worse.

We see, then, that trusting in politics to overcome your anxiety is not a new problem. It is an ancient one. But God has always had a different approach. As we will see, God has never called his people to disengage from the world, isolating themselves. But neither has God placed the hope of his people in any ruler, any nation, or any political movement. Instead, God has directed his people to look upward, take their anxieties to him, and humbly seek his face.

This was true for the exiles in Babylon. God, as we saw in Chapter 6, had further plans for his people, plans that extended far beyond the seventy years of their exile in Babylon. Jeremiah 29:11–14 indicated that the people were indeed politically sidelined, but they were not hopeless. Their hope was located in a remarkable new work of God, a work that would make the influence of Israel in its glory days seem a small thing.

God unfolded this promise in Jeremiah 31:33–34. In this passage, God shared with his people what he was going to do in the New Covenant era to come. God was not going to reestablish an Israelite theocracy. In the age of the New Covenant, he was going to form a people for himself from all across the world. This people would not receive his law from a mountaintop; they would receive his law in their hearts.

The prophet foretold all this:

> For this is the covenant that I will make with the house of Israel after those days, declares the LORD: I will put my law within them, and I will write it on their hearts.

> And I will be their God, and they shall be my people. And no longer shall each one teach his neighbor and each his brother, saying, "Know the LORD," for they shall all know me, from the least of them to the greatest, declares the LORD. For I will forgive their iniquity, and I will remember their sin no more. (Jeremiah 31:33–34)

The New Covenant meant a drastic change in God's dealing with man. The institution of the law and the revival of it during Josiah's reign had not led to national security or lasting holiness. As Jeremiah understood through God's gift of revelation, the people needed a new and better covenant.

Discussing Jeremiah's difficult ministry, Derek Kidner sums up this need: "But a third effect of his involvement in the reformation may have been even more far-reaching, for the experience revealed to him the inability of even the best of laws to reach the heart of a people for God. No attitudes had changed; only opportunities."[6]

The people were not to put their trust in politics and national solutions. After all, "The national covenant, like its original at Mount Sinai, was broken almost as soon as made. No experience could have prepared a prophet better to hear God's promise of a new and better covenant that would create a company of the converted and the era of the gospel."[7] Kidner is right: the people needed not a political cure, but a spiritual one. Just like us, they needed the gospel.

Our Greatest Need Is Spiritual, Not Political

The people needed something far stronger than the law. They needed God's moral truth, yes, but they needed lasting forgiveness secured by the blood of a greater sacrifice, a perfect and once-for-all sacrifice. They needed the transforming power of God's Spirit. They needed not an external code, good as that was, but an internal compulsion toward holiness and the glory of God that they did not have.

Though the people of God had wandered in the far country, they had hope. This is what Jeremiah 29, as well as Jeremiah 31—the New Covenant passage—together reveal: "the God who uproots does so not in cold anger but in painful love," as Andrew G. Shead has observed.[8] Babylon, it turned out, was not a dead-end. Babylon was a launchpad. Shead notes that as God draws near to his people,

> God promises to remake Israel from within by an act of forgiveness that amounts to drawing them into his own life, one by one. Such forgiveness cannot be confined within the boundaries of the old Israel, but spans the ruined world. So radical is this remaking of Israel that the whole fabric of the cosmos is caught up in it, and the age of the new covenant will, by virtue of a word of forgiveness, be the age of new creation, the age when death is no more.[9]

This is what God promised his people in Jeremiah 29 and 31. He was going to do something bigger than restoring the kingdom of Israel. That was what the people yearned for God to do; they wanted a political gospel that would guarantee political results. God, however, had something else up his sleeve. God wanted the whole earth to hear the gospel, for God wanted to gather a people from every tribe, tongue, and nation.

However, before God launched this new phase of the mission, he asked his people to do something we have always struggled to do: wait. The "age of the new covenant" would come, but not for over half a millennium. For many years, Babylon continued to flourish. Nebuchadnezzar the mighty king accrued tremendous wealth and gloried in his achievements. But great pride goes before a great fall.

As we see in Daniel 4:29–33, the great Nebuchadnezzar lost his kingship. The glory of Babylon did not endure. By 539 BC, Persia had conquered the country, bringing an end to Babylon's era of dominance. At this time, the prophecy of the exiles' return to Jerusalem came to fulfillment, as over 42,000 Jews initially left Babylon to go back under Zerubabbel's direction. In 458, 444, and 430 BC, successive waves of Jews returned to Jerusalem.

This return to David's city coincided with the close of the speech of God to his people in the Old Covenant era. No great takeover of Babylon, Persia, or the world had occurred. The people waited for the promises of God to come to fulfillment.

Jesus as the Hope of His People

This fulfillment came during the first century AD. God sent his Son, born of a virgin, God in human flesh. The ministry of Jesus represented the unfolding fulfillment of the Messianic promises. In the coming of Jesus, the mission of God to pagan peoples flowered in full. The gospel was unleashed; the cause of mercy and grace exploded in the world. Jesus, the Greater David and the true

Deliverer of his people, came to give his people rest from their works and their striving. The garden *shalom* that had so long evaded the people was within reach.

The New Testament presents us with the perfect fulfillment of this extraordinary operation. In a sense, the Father planted his Son in the greater Babylon. Jesus's entire coming was a mission of mercy. From the moment Jesus's ministry began, he showed in equivocal fashion that he was the one appointed by the Father to roll back the curse. Mark's Gospel catalogues this with almost breathless intensity. Here, for example, is an early scene in Mark's account in which Jesus met a man with an "unclean spirit":

> And he cried out, "What have you to do with us, Jesus of Nazareth? Have you come to destroy us? I know who you are—the Holy One of God." But Jesus rebuked him, saying, "Be silent, and come out of him!" And the unclean spirit, convulsing him and crying out with a loud voice, came out of him. And they were all amazed, so that they questioned among themselves, saying, "What is this? A new teaching with authority! He commands even the unclean spirits, and they obey him." And at once his fame spread everywhere throughout all the surrounding region of Galilee. (Mark 1:23b–28)

In moments like this, Jesus showed that he was indeed the Messiah. He was the long-promised Deliverer and King of his people. Satan was a terrible force on the earth, but Satan's minions proved no match for the Son of God. Facing a demon, Jesus rebuked him, commanded the unclean spirit to leave his host, and thus displayed his total command of the spiritual and physical realm. This exorcism symbolized the bigger purpose of Christ's coming, to exorcise Satan from the earth and liberate God's people from sin's tyranny.

This is exactly what Jesus accomplished on the cross. The Son of God fulfilled the purpose given him by the Father. At Calvary, he suffered and bled and died as a substitute sacrifice for his people. He died to satisfy the just wrath of God and to wash us clean of all our sins. He carried out a real and terrible death sentence on the devil, securing the defeat of Satan (1 John 3:8). In this way, he brought the atonement promises and themes of the Old Testament to glorious resolution, winning a people for himself, a people who can never be unsaved or unredeemed.[10]

After his vicarious resurrection three days after his death, Jesus returned to his disciples for a brief time. Just before he ascended to the right hand of the Father, Jesus gave his people their (and our) marching orders: the Great Commission of Matthew 28:18–20. The church was not to wage physical battle against unbelievers, antagonizing the lost. The church was to press into the darkness all around them, proclaiming the saving gospel, and making disciples of all who would repent and believe in Jesus, loving the lost.

This was not entirely what Jesus's followers wanted. In their weaker moments, they did not want a saving gospel; they wanted a political gospel. They wanted to push Caesar off the throne, reclaim the kingdom of Israel, and end their centuries of oppression and suffering. This hope persisted until the final seconds of Jesus's first coming. The disciples asked Jesus when he would establish his kingdom on the earth (see Acts 1:7). They failed to see that the death and resurrection of Jesus had secured total victory over a power far greater than Rome: Satan's own anti-kingdom.

Even as Jesus departed them, they *still* struggled to understand that the mission entrusted to them was a mission not of conquest, but of proclamation. The true king had come, but he did not call his people to take over the Babylon of their day (overthrowing Roman power), but to win lost souls to God. The mission to Babylon was no longer local; the mission to Babylon had gone global.

Honoring Caesar, Not Attacking Him: Jesus's Political Theology

Jesus had a greater mission for his people than taking political control of the world. Jesus called his people to go into all the world and rescue spiritual hostages of the devil, forming churches all across the globe. As he charged his disciples to carry out this great work, a far more significant work than any political endeavor, Jesus called his people to honor the state. So far from calling the church to overthrow Rome, Jesus taught that Caesar was a God-instituted authority.

The state, Jesus declared in no uncertain terms, had legitimate authority to rule and thus to issue taxes: "Therefore render to Caesar the things that are Caesar's, and to God the things that are God's" (Matthew 22:21). Instead of revoking Caesar's authority, Jesus reinforced it. He went so far as to identify taxes as "things that are Caesar's."

Then and now, these words hit like a thunderclap. They shatter the expectation of naïve disciples who think that following Jesus means opting out of submission to secular authority. Instead of such a move, Jesus taught that following him means *embracing* God-constituted authorities. This includes paying taxes, much as many of us yearn to be free of such duties.

Jesus did not bring a political gospel that overthrew Caesar. Instead, Jesus taught Christians to honor the state, submit to it as much as possible, and be a witnessing presence within it. But we should not make the mistake of thinking that Jesus cared nothing about this world, nor that he called his people to political quietism. He did no such thing; he called them to engage their context:

> You are the salt of the earth, but if salt has lost its taste, how shall its saltiness be restored? It is no longer good for anything except to be thrown out and trampled under people's feet. You are the light of the world. A city set on a hill cannot be hidden. Nor do people light a lamp and put it under a basket, but on a stand, and it gives light to all in the house. In the same way, let your light shine before others, so that they may see your good works and give glory to your Father who is in heaven. (Matthew 5:13–16)

In this glorious passage, we have the charge from Christ himself to be in the world but not of the world. By the power of God within us, we must produce "good works" that lead people to glorify God the Father. This means not a minimalist program of action but a comprehensive effort to be a force for good in all of life, private and public alike.

Scripture teaches us a holistic Christianity that brings as much gospel *shalom* to our modern Babylon as we can. Even as we do not make politics ultimate, neither do we render politics of no account. The same Gospel that saves us from the world calls us to go into the world. Matthew himself detailed the story of the courageous prophet John the Baptist as John challenged the sin of Herod and his sister-in-law. John did not hold back; he called out Herod's sin clearly, publicly, and continually (see Matthew 14:1–12).

For doing so, John the Baptist lost his head. Yet this first martyr for Christ left us no woebegone example. John the Baptist was a hero and summoned us to go and do likewise. We are not here to accommodate the world; we are here to proclaim God's truth in love to the world, come what may. In similar terms, Duane Garrett captures the connection between the Babylonian exiles and our role today:

> Seeking the peace and prosperity of Babylon means not living a subversive existence against the land in which you reside. . . . In the same manner [as the Jews], Christians are a community of "exiles" (1 Peter 1:1). They can build homes, raise children, start businesses, live lawfully, strive to be at peace with their neighbors, and serve patriotically in the land in which they reside. . . . But they must never forget that they have a higher citizenship. . . .[11]

Our existence in our country, in normal terms, is neither "subversive" nor ultimate. Our earthly citizenship comes second to our heavenly citizenship, for God is building the one true Christian nation, and it is composed of people from across the earth.

One Voice with Jesus: Paul and Peter on Church and State

This mission simply does not involve "Christianizing" government. Jesus offered no such mandate, nor did the Apostle Paul. In Romans 13:1–7, Paul urged the church in Rome to embrace God-given secular authority:

> Let every person be subject to the governing authorities. For there is no authority except from God, and those that exist have been instituted by God. Therefore whoever resists the authorities resists what God has appointed, and those who resist will incur judgment. For rulers are not a terror to good conduct, but to bad. Would you have no fear of the one who is in authority? Then do what is good, and you will receive his approval, for he is God's servant for your good. But if you do wrong, be afraid, for he does not bear the sword in vain. For he is the servant of God, an avenger who carries out God's wrath on the wrongdoer. Therefore one must be in subjection, not only to avoid God's wrath but also for the sake of conscience. For because of this you also pay taxes, for the authorities are ministers of God, attending to this very thing. Pay to all what is owed to them: taxes to whom taxes are owed, revenue to whom revenue is owed, respect to whom respect is owed, honor to whom honor is owed.

Instead of anarchy and rebellion in the name of Christ, Paul instructed the church in Rome (a noteworthy place) to "be subject" to the government. As much as is possible, the Christian submits to the government over them, for it is "instituted by God" (v. 1). The terms could not be clearer, much as we often wish the New Testament's political theology ran in other directions.

This is the longest teaching section on the state in the New Testament. It features no call to theonomy, no assertion that the state must fly the Christian flag, no call to Christianize the government. The political theology here is rather chastened and simple: rulers rule due to God's call. Christians submit to this rulership. Caesar wields the sword against evil, punishing it justly, carrying out nothing less than "God's wrath on the wrongdoer" (v. 4). Taxes are not inherently evil but are "owed" to the state (v. 7).

It is remarkable what is not found here. In our time, when many professing Christians have grown weary of feckless leadership, we see revived interest in theonomy and "Christian nationalism." In the above passage, we see that Paul gave no call to promote the adoption of the Old Covenant law in Rome. He communicated not a hint of theonomy nor a whisper of theocracy. Paul knew that Christ was king, but this kingship had a specific governing outpost: the church.

The Apostle Peter gave the same vision of public engagement as Jesus and Paul, as we see in 1 Peter 2:13–17:

> Be subject for the Lord's sake to every human institution, whether it be to the emperor as supreme, or to governors as sent by him to punish those who do evil and to praise

> those who do good. For this is the will of God, that by doing good you should put to silence the ignorance of foolish people. Live as people who are free, not using your freedom as a cover-up for evil, but living as servants of God. Honor everyone. Love the brotherhood. Fear God. Honor the emperor.

The emperor—who in Peter's day was likely Nero, a wicked tyrant—was "supreme" according to Peter (v. 13). Peter, we recall, knew no confusion about who was truly supreme in all things, yet here he esteemed the office of emperor and told believers to "honor" him (v. 17). Once again, we hear the summons to "be subject" to earthly rulership, for the state exists to punish evil and reward good (vss. 13–14).

This presentation does not mandate that believers obey unjust laws or set aside biblical teaching when Caesar requires this. We submit to Caesar with this proviso: *as much as is possible*, as stated above. But we simply cannot miss that the New Testament speaks with one voice in calling Christians to be good citizens in fallen countries.

What the Church Does and What Caesar Does

The New Testament may well surprise us in honoring the state. We might think that it would call us instead to political revolution in pursuit of national utopia. However, this straightforwardly is not what the New Testament teaches. Instead of calling for Caesar to be dethroned, for example, Peter directed Christians to honor the emperor as one bearing authority from God.

Our recognition of Caesar's authority does not equal an endorsement of Caesar's worldview. But Jesus, Paul, and Peter did not issue a summons to smash all neutrality and occupy all government offices. They did something much more chastened: they affirmed that Caesar has a God-given role in the world, even as they delineated what Caesar did from what the church did.

This is what Abraham Kuyper called "sphere sovereignty" over one hundred years ago.[12] Each of the God-made institutions, Kuyper argued, has its own jurisdiction. Just as Caesar has no charge from God to oversee corporate worship, elect pastors, and carry out church discipline, so the church has no summons from God to pick up the sword, hand down prison sentences, enact taxation codes, and condemn criminals. Each institution has its own charge from God; neither sphere (to use a synonymous term) should seize jurisdiction of the other.

Kuyper's biblical insight challenges an anxious and restless church. Again, we have been told by some that there is no neutrality in the cosmos. It is either "Christ or Chaos," and in the political realm, Caesar stands squarely in the "Chaos" camp. Yet I believe that this analysis suffers from some flaws. While it is true that the whole world lies under a spell of darkness, and that wicked rulers do harm the people of God, it is also true that God's common grace operates throughout our world.

Common grace is rarely talked about among Christians, surprisingly. But it is a big part of our lives and our world. In his common grace, God restrains evil, allows good to be done in this realm, and lets mankind enjoy life. Affirming a biblical conception of common grace in itself steers us away from an over-realized eschatology. God works through all sorts of people and means and entities and states to accomplish his purposes; it simply is not the case that God asks or expects us to function in a Christian-only bubble, obeying only Christian rulers, living under Christian laws alone, interacting with Christian people and no one else.

This sort of vision has caught on today. But it defies much of what Scripture depicts. As just one example of many, God works through secular rulers to help and even rescue his people. In Egypt, Pharoah appointed Joseph to a key leadership position, and the people of God received tremendous help through Joseph's wise governance. In Philistia, David was strangely spared by the very people he had helped Saul overcome, winning the favor of Philistine leadership for a season.

In Babylon, Daniel and his three young friends won favor from Nebuchadnezzar. They rose to positions of great prominence as Daniel became the king's wisest counselor. In Persia, King Artaxerxes both hindered and assisted the Jews, ultimately handing down the decree that allows the Jews to fight back against their would-be killers. So too did Cyrus of Persia permit Ezra and Nehemiah to rebuild Jerusalem. The overall point should be clear: the purposes of salvation are not infrequently entwined with the actions of the state.

In the New Testament era, the apostles did not ask a secular government to do their work. They did, however, profit from the Roman judicial system. When Paul was falsely accused, he appealed to Caesar on the basis of his Roman citizenship, displaying both a submission to Roman governance and a willingness to use its system for the advancement of the gospel (see Acts 22). At no point did Paul or any other biblical figure trust in the secular state to carry out God's mission. But we cannot miss that the Bible offers plenteous examples of unbelieving rulers—and governments—strangely lending help to the people of God.

In summary, here is what Scripture communicates to us about Christian involvement in the public square:

- We are not called to overthrow Caesar; we are called to pray for Caesar (1 Timothy 2:2).
- We are not urged to attack the emperor; we are urged to honor the emperor (1 Peter 2:17).
- We are not told to Christianize the government; we are called to support the state as it punishes evil and secondarily promotes good (Romans 13:1–7).
- We are not called to undermine the government; we are called to submit to the government as much as we can (1 Peter 2:13).
- We are not called to political radicalism and agitation; we are taught to lead a quiet life under the authority of our rulers (1 Timothy 2:2).
- We are not instructed to reject Caesar's taxation policies; we are instructed to abide by them (Matthew 22:21).
- Paul did not try to institute a new Christian theocracy in Acts; he used his Roman citizenship to extend his preaching ministry (Acts 22:25–28).

This thread of testimony helps us understand how we are to engage the rule of secular Caesar. We do not ask the state to be the church, nor the church to be the state. However, neither do we pretend that God never uses secular officials to assist his people. The hearts of kings are like a channel of water in his hand (see Proverbs 21:1), and in different times and seasons, he turns those channels to help his followers in special ways.

The Law Cannot Transform the Heart

Does all of this mean that Christians should endorse political "neutrality"? Should we conclude, in other words, that governments that promote biblical principles like religious liberty, ordered society, and state-driven justice will bring lasting peace on the earth? No, for as I have been at pains to say, our confidence does not rest in Caesar. To put it even stronger, our confidence *must not* rest in Caesar.

However, the "Christ or Chaos" vision taught by some seems to leave little room for God's common grace. Furthermore, just as neutrality is a fiction, so too is formal Christianization. It is not institutions or businesses or nations or governments that become Christian in the New Testament, after all. It is people who submit to Christ. It is people who have faith in Jesus, repent of their sins, and trust God to save them. It is people who then are baptized and join churches, taking the Lord's Supper as an expression of their faith commitment.

None of this means that we fail to try to influence our state and our culture. We should in fact be the best citizens of any in our community and nation. We should constantly seek the good of our neighbor out of love for our neighbor (see Matthew 22:34–39). We should strive to see as much evil pushed back, and as much goodness advanced, in our given place of calling. We are not indifferent to the world around us; we are here to be a gospel influence, and indeed, the gospel is always at the forefront of our public theology and our public engagement.

This emphasis on *gospel-driven public theology* is not sloganeering. It matters greatly. It is not that we are against the law; in the public square, we know that good laws matter, and so we contend for them. But we also know that laws will not change people's hearts. Old Testament Israel had laws aplenty, all of them from God, and all of them good. But law did not keep Israel in check. Law has no power to transform, and law did not prevent Israel's stumbling.

As Jeremiah foresaw, we live in the age of New Covenant Christianity. The New Covenant concerns itself not with public administration of nations, but with the regeneration of the heart. This has great import for us today. We pray for leaders to rule well (see 1 Timothy 2:2), but we know that only the gospel will save sinners. Therefore, the more the gospel spreads, the stronger our communities—and country—may well be (at least for a time). Evangelical public theology speaks to many issues, but it always goes back to the gospel message.

Jesus Will Make the World Right

It should be clear by this point that waiting on Jesus does not look like laziness in Jesus's name. The apostles were not exactly dormant in the days after Jesus ascended to glory. But we mark their example well. As I said above, they made no attempt to reinstate ancient Israel, nor to conquer pagan nations. Instead, they taught the church of its true identity: we are “sojourners and exiles” on the earth (1 Peter 2:11).

Yet here we must slip in one of Scripture’s many surprising comments on our current state. Even as we seek the eternal resting place where heaven meets earth, we who are presently exiles are the dwelling-place of God. It is not the church building that is God’s habitation. It is not a governmental edifice with Corinthian columns that is God’s current abode. It is God’s people who are indwelt by the Spirit, and thus rendered a temple—the site of God’s special presence—in the age of the New Covenant (see 1 Corinthians 6:19).

Knowing this, we are not to try and make any one place the lasting location of the Lord. Much as we might like to make a permanent base for God on the earth, the author of Hebrews steers us away from such an instinct. Knowing what Christ has done, “let us go to him outside the camp and bear the reproach he endured. For here we have no lasting city, but we seek the city that is to come” (Hebrews 13:13–14).

This last sentence has explosive implications for how we construe our mission. We all desire our exile to end. This is not only an acceptable emotion, but a righteous emotion. We are not home. We have not arrived at the place of our eternal rest. While we have every blessing secured in the heavenly places through the finished work of Christ, we await the final realization of that blessing in eternity.

Just as we cannot build a lasting city, so we cannot build a lasting nation in our own strength. In distinction from the claims of Christian Nationalism that we addressed earlier, 1 Peter 2:9

teaches us that there is already a Christian nation on the earth. It is composed of every believer, for all the people of God are "a chosen race, a royal priesthood, a holy nation, a people for his own possession, that you may proclaim the excellencies of him who called you out of darkness into his marvelous light."

This verse matters greatly for Christian political theology—and for a happy and healthy walk with Christ in everyday terms. The only nation that will last forever is the one that Peter identifies, the "holy nation" of God. This is a nation that no one can add to by human cleverness, nor anyone destroy by human malevolence. This is not a nation that we build; this is not a project that we must anxiously, even obsessively, steward. This is the nation that God is building by his own hands.

Conclusion

We live in an anxious age. This is not only true of others; it is true of we ourselves. In the political realm, we long for things to be made right. However, as we have seen, God has not directed us to *Christianize* the world. Instead, we should *cultivate* our world. That is, as we have addressed above, we should bring light to dark places. We should love our neighbor. We should promote truth, righteousness, and the gospel in the public square.

A cultivation mindset drives us to be as influential as we can be in the public square. It summons us to courage, action, and proclamation. After all, we do not want our civilization to fall; just like the exiles in Babylon, we want to bring *shalom* to it. However, a cultivation mindset is distinct from a conquering mindset. We are not the ones who can make the world right. Only Jesus can.

In a time of great anxiety, we return to this truth: our hope is in *Christ*. Even if worse comes to worst, Jesus will not fail us. We are a part of the nation that will endure beyond all time, the "holy nation" that is in Christ. Knowing this, we need not fear the world or try to repair it in our own strength. We need to trust God and regularly lift our eyes to the hills. From there comes our help until the day that Christ comes on the clouds.

CONCLUSION

Toward Greater Gardens

The story of the Babylonian exiles that we have traced in these pages reminds me of pottery. Firstly, it reminds me of how precious things break. We can all recall a past situation, perhaps from childhood, when we unintentionally damaged a precious family heirloom. A game of tag got a little out of hand, or perhaps a tennis ball found its way into a forbidden living room, and next thing you know, a one-hundred-year-old family keepsake took on a new identity in the form of a thousand different pieces on the floor.

Things fall apart in our fallen world. So it was for Israel and Judah. As we have seen, these once-great tribes shattered into a thousand pieces. The Babylonian exile represented a nadir, a low point, for Judah. After years of putting up with the idolatry of his people, God acted and sent them into exile, placing them under the rule of a pagan king. The dream of Israel—a united kingdom imaging the glory of God on the earth in intentional form—died.

Yet this is where a second element of pottery comes to mind. Years ago, I learned of a most remarkable form of art. It is Japanese, and it is called *kintsugi*, meaning "to join with gold." Kintsugi craftsmanship deals exclusively with one kind of item: broken ones. You cannot practice this art form with pristine pots or bowls; you can only practice it with items that have broken, shattered, and scattered.

This artform is not a quick-dry endeavor. It takes weeks, months, and even years to recreate a broken vessel. The artist must be fully committed to the task, spending costly hours assembling pieces before beginning to unite them with gold lacquer. In *kintsugi*, the artist remakes just a single piece of houseware, rebuilding it one shard at time, working to form the whole as they recreate each portion with painstaking precision.

Here is the remarkable reality of this process, however. It is not about creating from scratch. It is entirely a work of recreation or new creation. The pot that is rebuilt once existed; it was a valued pot. In *kintsugi*, that pot is reconstructed, but it is not merely restored. It is altogether recrafted. Bearing striated gold lines across it, the pot has become more beautiful, and far more valuable, than it was in its original form.

The God Who Makes Broken Things Beautiful

I thought of *kintsugi* as I considered the story of Judah, and even more broadly, the story of this world. As we saw earlier, Judah fell. It broke. Yet God did a new work in and through the exile to Babylon. Instead of sweeping the shattered remnant of his people away, God sent his people into a pagan city. He did so not to punish them, ultimately, but to use them to bless Babylon, and reach it with the light of his truth.

In time, as we saw in Chapter 7, this meant not merely a local mission to Babylon, but a global mission of the gospel to the ends of the earth. God used the fall of Israel and Judah to inaugurate the ministry of the New Covenant, a ministry that continues to reach across the world. This work will continue until the end of the age, when the whole world will be made right in the perfect timing of God.

The story of God's redeeming work reminds me of Makoto Fujimura's eloquent reflections on the redeeming nature of *kintsugi*. "In Kintsugi," Fujimura writes, "Japanese Urushi (lacquer) is made from poison sumac. A poisonous tree of the fall is turned into a medium through which Kintsugi mending is done."[1] Through the transforming power of the master-artist, "Beauty can arise out of the ashes, and beauty can arise out of (as in Kintsugi) the curse of brokenness."[2]

So it is with the Redeemer God of Scripture. God is the Creator, but not only this. God is also the Re-Creator. He takes what is poisonous, a cross designed to kill, and uses it for the greatest possible good, complete atonement for the sins of his people. He does the same in the daily details of our fragile, often challenging lives, using our brokenness, our pain, our difficult relationships, and our ongoing trials to make us into a beautiful work of "new creation."

God, we see, is the original *kintsugi* artist. Though the beauty of this place has suffered grave attack from a terrible foe, Satan does not own this realm, nor control it. He operates within it (see

Job 1), but God is the one who owns all the pottery (see Romans 9). God is the one, furthermore, who undertakes the intricate work of renewing sinners like us, and of remaking a world like ours.

Time Itself Will Be Redeemed

The story of God's people mirrors the story of this world. This realm is fallen, and everything around us is subject to the reign of sin. However, in God's perfect plan, the world will not stay as it is. When Jesus makes all things right, he will not simply restore the world to Edenic conditions. When Jesus makes all things right, he will render the world far more beautiful than it ever was—more beautiful even than the paradise of the first garden.

Andrew Peterson speaks to the glory that awaits we who now garden under the shadow of the curse:

> [W]e priests of the New Creation will be clothed immortal to reign over our own gardens, and we'll do it without the specter of Death hovering over it all, taunting us with the sorrow of Time and the lie of futility. Glory be to God. Time itself will be redeemed, because it will no longer be an adversary, but a friend, an everlasting Sabbath, an unending feast.[3]

As Peterson captures, the redemption we will experience will be so full, so pervasive, so all-encompassing that "Time itself will be redeemed." We will no longer fight the clock; we will no longer labor under deadlines; we will no longer feel a strange mix of fevered anxiety and deep exhaustion by all that we have left undone each day. Instead, we will live in "everlasting Sabbath," perpetual rest, unbroken peace.

A day will come when we will feel the last burst of chaos, navigate the last flutter of uncertainty, and get hit by the last dose of fear. We will feel these things, as we have felt them so many times as fallen creatures, and then—in the twinkling of an eye—we will never feel them again. Everlasting Sabbath will begin.

This will not owe to therapy. It will not come because of any medication. It will not result from a more positive "me-centered" mindset. It will not flow from embracing our raw desires and being affirmed by the people around us. Our complete healing, the resolution of everything that goes awry within us and around us, will spring directly from the work of God in its final form. Then, we will face no evil thing and will experience every good thing. *Shalom.*

Until that day, we have *garden hunger.* Our desire for a place of lasting and unbreakable solace will not go away. As we have noted, there is no way to silence this yearning of the soul. There is no method that can quiet these desires of the heart. We were made for God, and we were made for gardens. As long as we live in a fallen place, a realm that groans under the weight of the curse (see Romans 8:22), we sojourn as exiles.

But soon—even very soon—we will be home.

The New Eden Is Coming

We will find our Lord and Savior there. He is awaiting us now, and he will soon welcome us into the mountain garden-city that is the New Jerusalem, the city that covers the whole earth, as the Apostle John saw:

> Then the angel showed me the river of the water of life, bright as crystal, flowing from the throne of God and of the Lamb through the middle of the street of the city; also, on either side of the river, the tree of life with its twelve kinds of fruit, yielding its fruit each month. The leaves of the tree were for the healing of the nations. No longer will there be anything accursed, but the throne of God and of the Lamb will be in it, and his servants will worship him. They will see his face, and his name will be on their foreheads. And night will be no more. They will need no light of lamp or sun, for the Lord God will be their light, and they will reign forever and ever. (Revelation 22:1–5)

Just as the tree of life was found in Eden, so it is found in the New Eden. In this mountain garden-city, the tree of life bears continual fruit, just as the first Eden teemed with life and yielded a delicious harvest. Everything the first Eden had, the New Eden has in greater form, and all without any possibility of sin or attack or ruination. This is a city of total calm. It will feel perfectly stable and secure, for it is indeed God's own city. It does not even need the sun, for God himself lights the streets of this place.

It is in this city that our *garden hunger* will end. In that place, we who experienced the shattering effects of our sin will experience the fullness of wholeness. Like a *kintsugi* pot, we will be more beautiful than we once were; we will be not only a recreation, but a wholly healed new creation. All of our waiting will be worth it; all of our cultivation will come to fruition.

The desert will bloom, our anxiety will end, and we will dwell forever in the place where heaven meets earth and the soul meets God.

Acknowledgments

I am grateful to God for the opportunity to write this humble book. At the human level, the support of my wife, Bethany, has meant everything to me. Without her, I could not write. My children have supported me throughout with good cheer and kind words; it brings me special joy that my daughter, Ella, created the cover art for this book. Ella herself is a cultivator of no small skill, and her mother and I are so very proud of her.

A Call to Cultivate is dedicated to Ryan Carr. Ryan is a faithful and very gifted man whose ability in his craft is matched only by his humility before the Lord. He is a great friend, a brother-at-arms, and a continual source of encouragement to me. In addition, he has helped me develop a working vision for my basketball team's offense, which is no small gift.

I am very thankful for Skyhorse Publishing, led by Tony Lyons, a principled advocate of free speech. At Skyhorse, my editor,

Kathryn Riggs, has backed this project for years. Since 2022, when I first proposed this book to her, she has not only seen my vision for this book—a mildly unusual one, I must admit—but has sharpened, clarified, and improved my articulation of this vision. Kathryn is an excellent editor and a much-appreciated colleague.

In my daily vocation, I have the joy of laboring alongside Jon Benzinger as we develop One Gospel for God's glory. Jon is a very dear friend, as is Dale Thackrah. The Redeemer Bible Church of Gilbert team (and congregation) is a serious blessing to me, as is Clifton Baptist Church of Louisville, Kentucky.

My interest in reading and writing began while growing up in the house of Andy and Donna Strachan. I am so thankful for my father and mother, and my sister, Rachel Burgess, and her family (Lester and Carter). I give thanks to God for my in-laws, Bruce and Jodi Ware, as well as my sister-in-law Rachel Ware. My family is a great source of encouragement and help to me.

About the Author

Owen Strachan is the Director and Cofounder of One Gospel. He has published over twenty books, including the bestselling *Christianity and Wokeness*, *Reenchanting Humanity*, *The War on Men*, and *The Warrior Savior.* Prior to his current work, Strachan led the Culture Center for the James Dobson Family Institute and taught systematic theology for several schools, including Midwestern Seminary and the Southern Baptist Theological Seminary.

A native of coastal Maine, Strachan is married to Bethany and is the father of three children. He speaks regularly at churches and conferences and hosts two popular podcasts: *Reenchant* (on his personal Substack) and the *One Gospel* podcast. In his free time, he enjoys coaching youth basketball, watching Westerns, traveling to beautiful places with his family, eating scones, and reading about Winston Churchill.

Strachan is active on X (@ostrachan), Instagram (@profstrachan), and Facebook. He hosts a popular podcast and hosts his regular content on his Substack, *Reenchant with Owen Strachan*, at owenstrachan.substack.com.

About One Gospel

One Gospel is a content resource ministry with a vertical focus. Founded in 2025 and anchored at Redeemer Bible Church (Gilbert, Arizona), we seek to lift the church's gaze to God through articles, podcast episodes, videos, books, conferences, and more.

Our ministry has three major emphases:

1. Build a Christian worldview for the rising generation anchored in the gospel
2. Offer gracious Reformed theology driven by the gospel
3. Unify believers fractured by tribalism through the gospel

One Gospel is led by Owen Strachan, Director, and Jon Benzinger, Senior Pastor of Redeemer Bible Church of Gilbert, Arizona.

You are warmly invited to engage our work at onegospel.net.

About *Reenchant with Owen Strachan*

Reenchant with Owen Strachan equips Christians to "reenchant" a lost world by engaging it with the grace and truth of Jesus Christ (see John 1:17). Strachan's Substack features regular written articles and a unique podcast. Subscribe to this content by visiting owen-strachan.substack.com.

Notes

Introduction

1 C. S. Lewis, *Surprised by Joy* (Orlando: Harcourt, 1955), 15. For further context, see the helpful discussion in Alister McGrath, *C. S. Lewis: A Life* (Carol Stream: Tyndale House, 2013), 18–20.
2 Lewis, *Surprised by Joy*, 69.
3 Andrew Peterson, *The God of the Garden: Thoughts on Creation, Culture, and the Kingdom* (Nashville: B&H, 2021), 198.
4 Augustine, *Confessions*, translated by Henry Chadwick (Oxford: Oxford University Press, 2008), 1.1.1 (3).
5 Ana Miller, "Can This Marriage Be Saved?," Science Watch—American Psychological Association, April 2013, https://www.apa.org/monitor/2013/04/marriage.
6 Karen Doyle, "Here's How Often Americans Move—and How Much They're Spending," Yahoo Finance, December 29, 2023, https://finance.yahoo.com/news/often-americans-move-much-spending-160007108.html.
7 Bureau of Labor Statistics, "Number of Jobs, Labor Market Experience, Marital Status, and Health for Those Born 1957–1964," August 26, 2025, https://www.bls.gov/news.release/pdf/nlsoy.pdf.

8 Thom Rainer, "The Dangerous Third Year of Pastoral Tenure," Church Answers, June 18, 2014, https://churchanswers.com/blog/dangerous-third-year-pastoral-tenure.

9 Melanie Hanson, "College Dropout Rates," Education Data Initiative, July 7, 2025, https://educationdata.org/college-dropout-rates#:~:text=First%2Dtime%20full%2Dtime%20undergraduate,income%20than%20bachelor's%20degree%20holders.

10 National Association of Realtors, "First-Time Home Buyer Share Falls to Historic Low of 21%, Median Age Rises to 40," November 4, 2025, https://www.nar.realtor/newsroom/first-time-home-buyer-share-falls-to-historic-low-of-21-median-age-rises-to-40.

11 Aimee Picchi and Mary Cunningham, "America's Deepening Affordability Crisis Summed Up in 5 Charts," CBS News, November 19, 2025, https://www.cbsnews.com/news/affordability-2025-inflation-food-prices-housing-child-care-health-costs.

12 Joyce Chen, "CEO Tenure Rates," Harvard Law School Forum on Corporate Governance, August 4, 2023, https://corpgov.law.harvard.edu/2023/08/04/ceo-tenure-rates-2.

13 Shayna Goldman, "NHL Coach Hiring Trends, by the Numbers: How Many Retreads? Longest Tenures?," *The Athletic*, May 9, 2025, https://www.nytimes.com/athletic/6343534/2025/05/09/nhl-coaches-joel-quenneville-mike-sullivan.

14 Steve Madeley and William Jones, "How Premier League Manager Exits and Tenures Compare to NFL, NBA, NHL and MLB," *The Athletic*, May 23, 2024, https://www.nytimes.com/athletic/5509303/2024/05/23/premier-league-manager-sackings-nfl-nba.

15 Kamile Viezelyte, "Juggling Security: How Many Passwords Does the Average Person Have in 2024?," NordPass, April 24, 2024, https://nordpass.com/blog/how-many-passwords-does-average-person-have.

16 American Psychological Association, "APA Poll Reveals a Nation Suffering from Stress of Societal Division, Loneliness," November 6, 2025, https://www.apa.org/news/press/releases/2025/11/nation-suffering-division-loneliness.

17 Jonathan Haidt, *The Anxious Generation: How the Great Rewiring of Childhood Is Causing an Epidemic of Mental Illness* (New York: Penguin, 2024), 12.

18 Ibid., 31. The data is from the US Centers for Disease Control, National Center for Injury Prevention and Control.

19 Haidt, *The Anxious Generation*, 33.

20 Naman Trivedi, "TikTok's Viral 'ChatGPT Devil Trend' Explained After Rice Student Claire Tracy's Death: 'The Devil Couldn't Reach Me'," Times Now, December 13, 2025, https://www.timesnownews.com/world/us/us-news/tiktoks-viral-chatgpt-devil-trend-explained-after-rice-university-student-claire-tracys-death-the-devil-couldnt-reach-me-article-153285281.

21 See Ibram X. Kendi, *How to Be an Antiracist* (New York: One World, 2019); Robin DiAngelo, *White Fragility: Why It's So Hard for White People to Talk about Racism* (Boston: Beacon Press, 2018). For a helpful economic response, see Thomas Sowell, *Discrimination and Disparities* (New York: Hachette, 2019); along biblical lines, I gave a gospel-shaped response to wokeness in Owen Strachan, *Christianity and Wokeness: How the Social Justice Movement Is Hijacking the Gospel—and the Way to Stop It* (Washington, DC: Salem Books, 2021).

22 For more on these trends and the biblical response to them, see Owen Strachan, *The War on Men: Why Society Hates Them and Why We Need Them* (Washington, DC: Salem, 2023).

23 I responded to the modern "disenchanted" vision of the human person in Owen Strachan, *Reenchanting Humanity: A Theology of Mankind* (Fearn, Scotland: Christian Focus, 2019). *Reenchanting Humanity* is a kind of companion volume to the current book; this book complements and builds off of the biblical anthropology of the former title.

24 Alliance for Responsible Citizenship, "The Poet Who Made 500,000 People Cry | Joshua Luke Smith," February 19, 2025, https://www.youtube.com/watch?v=fsiB9uCMZ68. The video has over 520,000

views. The extended lines are used with permission from Smith, for which I am grateful.

25 John Calvin, *Institutes of the Christian Religion* (1541), translated by Robert White (Edinburgh: Banner of Truth, 2014), 1.1 (2).

26 Jonathan Edwards, *The End for Which God Created the World*, Yale Works of Jonathan Edwards, Volume 8 (New Haven: Yale University Press, 1989 [1765]), 531. A more beautiful paragraph than this one can scarcely find. To learn more about Edwards and his theology, consult the writings of John Piper. A gifted and faithful pastor-theologian, Piper has been for many years the foremost expositor of Edwards's "theocentric" theology. See especially John Piper, *Desiring God: Meditations of a Christian Hedonist*, Revised Edition (Wheaton: Crossway, 2025 [1986]); also Owen Strachan and Douglas Sweeney, *The Essential Jonathan Edwards: An Introduction to the Life and Teaching of America's Greatest Theologian* (Chicago: Moody, 2018); Owen Strachan, *Always in God's Hands: Day by Day in the Company of Jonathan Edwards* (Carol Stream: Tyndale House, 2018).

Chapter 1

1 If you can, I encourage you to visit the Cohn Family Butterfly Pavilion at the Desert Botanical Garden in Phoenix. It is well worth the trip, as is the outdoor butterfly garden at Chartwell, the estate once owned by Winston Churchill in Kent, England. These are the two such sites that I have visited as an amateur enthusiast.

2 Katie Roiphe, "Why Are So Many Women Dreaming of Rustic Domesticity?," *Wall Street Journal*, December 4, 2025, https://www.wsj.com/style/design/why-are-so-many-women-dreaming-of-rustic-domesticity.

3 Brought to prominence under the reign of Hammurabi (who ruled from 1792–1750 BC), Babylon is mentioned around four hundred times in the Bible. In the New Testament, particularly the Book of Revelation, Babylon is a shorthand for the wicked populace led by Satan that opposes the people of God (see Revelation 17–18, e. g.).

For more context, consult B. T. Arnold, "Babylon," in *New Dictionary of Biblical Theology: Exploring the Unity & Diversity of Scripture*, eds. T. Desmond Alexander, Brian S. Rosner, D. A. Carson, and Graeme Goldsworthy (Downers Grove, Illinois: InterVarsity, 2000), 392–93.

4 At the very time that the exiles of Judah entered the city, in fact, Babylon's economy grew exponentially. According to Hans Barstad, "In the Neo-Babylonian period [including Nebuchadnezzar's reign], the introduction of camel caravans benefited overland trade considerably. During the Neo-Babylonian Period, trade became ever more wide-reaching. International trade with Asia Minor, Syria, Phoenicia, Cyprus, Greece, Egypt, and Elam flourished." Hans M. Barstad, "The City-State of Jerusalem in the Neo-Babylonian Empire: Evidence from the Surrounding States," in John J. Ahn and Jill Middlemas, eds., *By the Irrigation Canals of Babylon: Approaches to the Study of Exile* (London: T&T Clark), 37.

5 Andrew George, "A Tour of Nebuchadnezzar's Babylon," in I. L. Finkel and M. J. Seymour, eds., *Babylon* (Oxford: Oxford University Press, 2009), 54.

6 Babylon was less an open metropolis like modern meta-cities and more "a fortress of which the inhabited part was surrounded and protected by the encircling girdle of the walls," according to leading archaeologist Robert Koldewey. See Robert Koldewey, *The Excavations at Babylon* (London: Macmillan, 1914), 5. Entering Babylon would have felt less like going to the mall and more like walking into a massive military establishment, albeit with a highly developed market exchange system.

7 Arnold, "Babylon," 394.

8 Babylon's impressive culture influences us to the current day. Our chronology and geometry alike derive from the sixty-second minute, sixty-minute hour, and the 360-degree circle used in Babylonian measurements. See I. L. Finkel and M. J. Seymour, eds., *Babylon* (Oxford: Oxford University Press, 2009), 192.

9 Ibid, 394.

10 See the helpful survey of the pre-exile period in Derek Kidner, *The Message of Jeremiah*, The Bible Speaks Today (Downers Grove, Illinois: InterVarsity, 1987), 16.

11 Philip Graham Ryken, *Jeremiah and Lamentations: Sorrow and Hope, Preaching the Word* (Wheaton: Crossway, 2001), 409.

12 Walter C. Kaiser Jr. and Tiberius Rata, *Walking the Ancient Paths: A Commentary on Jeremiah* (Lexham: Bellingham, Washington, 2019), 331.

13 Joni Eareckson Tada, "Reflections on the 50th Anniversary of My Diving Accident," The Gospel Coalition, July 30, 2017, https://www.thegospelcoalition.org/article/reflections-on-50th-anniversary-of-my-diving-accident.

14 C. S. Lewis, *The Problem of Pain* (San Francisco: HarperCollins, 2001 [1940]), 88–89.

Chapter 2

1 Aristotle, *Politics*, translated by Benjamin Jowett (Kitchener, Ontario: Batoche, 1999 [circa 323 BC]), 3.1.12 (54), cited in I. L. Finkel and M. J. Seymour, eds., *Babylon* (Oxford: Oxford University Press, 2009), 115.

2 See Joshua J. Mark, "Trade in Ancient Mesopotamia," World History, November 22, 2022, https://www.worldhistory.org/article/2114/trade-in-ancient-mesopotamia.

3 There were roughly four or five walls protecting the southern palace of Nebuchadnezzar from the outside world, a detail that speaks to the architectural solidity and military might of Babylon. See Finkel and Seymour, eds., *Babylon*, 115.

4 Koldewey, *The Excavations at Babylon*, 196.

5 To underscore Marduk's significance, the temple priests took the statue out on occasion, and paraded it through Babylon, reminding the city of the god's centrality. See Andre Parrot, *Babylon and the Old Testament*, Studies in Biblical Archaeology, Number 8 (New York: Philosophical Society, 1956), 53.

6 Historian Georges Contenau pictures the average Babylonian house as closed off from the outside world, though situated in a teeming meta-city: "the door affords the only entry for light and air from the outside world. . . . The house is, in short, simply a box built without foundations upon levelled and beaten earth. Bricks are used when they are three-quarters dry, and are bonded with mortar made of diluted clay which, when it dries, makes a wall of uniform strength." Georges Contenau, *Everyday Life in Babylon and Assyria* (London: Edward Arnold, 1959), 28. The interiority of the individual Babylonian home mirrored the interiority of the city itself.

7 Facts and Details, "Ancient Mesopotamian Homes," July 2024, https://africame.factsanddetails.com/article/entry-1001.html.

8 Duane A. Garrett, *Understanding Jeremiah: Its Setting, Composition, and Message* (Grand Rapids: Kregel, 2025), 223.

Chapter 3

1 The Butchart Gardens, "See Our Story," The Butchart Gardens, https://butchartgardens.com/our-story.

2 This calling would have resonated with Jeremiah himself, as well. Andrew G. Shead helpfully notes that Jeremiah's original commission, given in the opening verses of this lengthy book, was "to build and to plant" (1:10). From that starting point come "small oracles of hope bobbing on the ride of destruction that sweeps through the first half of the book." Andrew G. Shead, *A Mouth Full of Fire: The Word of God in the Words of Jeremiah*, New Studies in Biblical Theology 29 (Downers Grove: InterVarsity, 2012), 187. The commission of Jeremiah related to the calling of the exiles; in both cases, God wanted planting, not privation, and faithfulness, not fearfulness.

3 Contenau, *Everyday Life in Babylon and Assyria*, 48.

4 Primarily because I struggle to believe that the Greeks simply invented this matter, and also because the Babylonians were master-creators in many respects.

5 Have you tried remembering your password for one of your seventeen two-step authentication accounts recently? If so, would you honestly describe that experience as "simple"?
6 Francis Schaeffer, *Art and the Bible* (Downers Grove, Illinois: InterVarsity, 2006 [1973]), 26.
7 Ibid., 27.
8 This allows us to redefine the artist as well. A true artist is not one who fussily makes things that few understand and only the avant-garde appreciate. A true artist works for God's honor, creating beauty that all can appreciate, applying skillful labor to enhance their surroundings. All this is a reflection of the original artist, God, who did not make a drably functional planet, but filled this earth with life and beauty and wonder.
9 Martin Luther, *Works of Martin Luther* 19 (Shriften 1526), *Weimarer Ausgabe* (657). See Gustaf Wingren, *Luther on the Doctrine of Vocation* (Eugene, Oregon: Wipf and Stock, 1957), 3–4.
10 John MacArthur, "Taking the Mystery Out of Knowing God's Will," sermon preached at Grace Community Church, March 24, 2017, https://www.youtube.com/watch?v=SGnHAqu9Geo. See also this excellent short book: John MacArthur, *Found: God's Will* (Colorado Springs: David C. Cook, 2012).
11 C. S. Lewis, "They Asked for a Paper," in *Is Theology Poetry?* (London: Geoffrey Bless, 1962), 164–65.
12 Daniel Dustin worked on radar during World War II. A graduate of Bates College (I went to rival Bowdoin), he was MIT-trained, flew to Washington regularly for high-level governmental meetings he never talked about, and served Grace Chapel for years as an elder. I look forward to seeing him again when God calls me home; I have missed him ever since he died.
13 Peterson, *The God of the Garden*, 117.
14 Ibid, 118–19.
15 Ibid, 192–93.
16 Philip Graham Ryken, *Jeremiah and Lamentations: Sorrow and Hope, Preaching the Word* (Wheaton: Crossway, 2001), 414.

Chapter 4

1 Grant Bailey, Lyman Stone, and Brad Wilcox, "Divorce in Decline: About 40% Of Today's Marriages Will End in Divorce," Institute for Family Studies, July 24, 2025, https://ifstudies.org/blog/divorce-in-decline-about-40-of-todays-marriages-will-end-in-divorce.

2 Benjamin Gurrentz, "Unmarried Partners More Diverse Than 20 Years Ago," Census.gov, September 23, 2019, https://www.census.gov/library/stories/2019/09/unmarried-partners-more-diverse-than-20-years-ago.html.

3 Mike Stobbe, "The U.S. Fertility Rate Reached a New Low in 2024, CDC Data Shows," PBS Newshour, July 24, 2025, https://www.pbs.org/newshour/nation/the-u-s-fertility-rate-reached-a-new-low-in-2024-cdc-data-shows.

4 Richard Fry, "A Record-High Share of 40-Year-Olds in the U.S. Have Never Been Married," Pew Research, June 28, 2023, https://www.pewresearch.org/short-reads/2023/06/28/a-record-high-share-of-40-year-olds-in-the-us-have-never-been-married.

5 Jeffrey M. Jones, "LGBTQ+ Identification in U.S. Rises to 9.3%," Gallup, February 20, 2025, https://news.gallup.com/poll/656708/lgbtq-identification-rises.aspx.

6 National Right to Life, "Abortion Statistics: United States Data and Trends," January 2022, https://www.nrlc.org/uploads/factsheets/FS01AbortionintheUS.pdf.

7 Jack Lundbom, *Jeremiah 21–36*, The Anchor Yale Bible 21b (New Haven: Yale University Press, 2004), 351.

8 Contenau, *Everyday Life in Babylon and Assyria*, 15.

9 Joshua J. Mark, "The Family in Ancient Mesopotamia," World History Encyclopedia, September 27, 2022, https://www.worldhistory.org/article/16/the-family-in-ancient-mesopotamia.

10 Mark Oliver, "By the Rivers of Babylon: Life in Ancient Babylon's Thriving Jewish Community," Ancient Origins, May 9, 2018, https://www.ancient-origins.net/history-important-events/rivers-babylon-life-ancient-babylon-s-thriving-jewish-community-0010021.

11 J. A. Thompson, *The Book of Jeremiah*, The New International Commentary on the Old Testament (Grand Rapids: Eerdmans, 1980), 285.

12 Kidner makes the chilling point that pagan forms of worship had so influenced the Jews that even "children" participated "in its pleasant routines." Kidner, *The Message of Jeremiah*, 133.

13 Many Christian approaches to lust omit the targeting of our sinful desires, emphasizing instead our actions. For a desire-focused approach to defeating lust (for both men and women), see Owen Strachan and Gavin Peacock, *What Does the Bible Teach About Lust?* (Fearn, Scotland: Christian Focus, 2020).

14 To read more about biblical complementarity, see John Piper and Wayne Grudem, eds., *Recovering Biblical Manhood & Womanhood: A Response to Evangelical Feminism* (Wheaton: Crossway, 2006 [1991]); Edith Schaeffer, *The Hidden Art of Homemaking* (Carol Stream: Tyndale House, 1985); Elisabeth Elliot, *Let Me Be a Woman* (Carol Stream: Tyndale House, 1999 [1976]); Herman Bavinck, *The Christian Family*, trans. Nelson D. Kloosterman (Grand Rapids: Christian's Library Press, 2012); Owen Strachan and Gavin Peacock, *The Grand Design: Male and Female He Made Them* (Fearn, Scotland: Christian Focus, 2016).

15 I will respond to these ideas in rapid-fire form. No, the sexes are not unequal before God; no, women are not inferior to men, nor are men inferior to women; I do not believe that men should "rule" their wives, but lovingly lead them; men should not demand submission from their wives; girls have complete freedom to go to college, should they want to do so; we have no biblical mandate to have a certain number of children, and much of this conversation depends on a woman's frame, capacity, and health; men should definitely apologize to their families when they sin, as doing so actually strengthens their leadership; women are indeed more emotionally complex than men, but this in no way means that women cannot think well, offer great counsel, and feel truth at the emotional level; conflict resolution requires both spouses to search their hearts regarding sin, with men

sometimes holding back confession, and women sometimes struggling to forgive; women are completely free in biblical terms to vote in both church and society, and this is no threat to male leadership; men are not "pastors" of their homes, and are free to lead the family in worship as works best for the family.

Again, a number of these stances will come—for some Christians—from a sincere desire to please God and build a godly life. That is commendable. However, we must take care that we do not concretize our own practice as binding on all believers. It is all too easy to take a principle that may genuinely work for our family and then codify it as a new moral law for all Christian families. While always pursuing wisdom and learning from others, we must take care that we guard the freedom of the gospel and fight against the legalistic impulses of our heart.

16 Quoted from Austin's Blog, "Paul Washer on Marriage," June 7, 2016, https://austind90.org/2016/06/07/paul-washer-on-marriage.

Chapter 5

1 Samuel McKoy, "The Tophet—Where Israelites Sacrificed Their Children?," Armstrong Institute of Biblical Archaeology, January/February 2025, https://armstronginstitute.org/1182-the-tophet-where-israelites-sacrificed-their-children.

2 Ryken, *Jeremiah and Lamentations*, 411.

3 Kidner, *The Message of Jeremiah*, 100.

4 Kaiser and Rata, *Walking the Ancient Paths*, 332.

5 This is the phrase used by Kaiser and Rata (331), and it is an apt one. Revolution comes by way of ordinary faithfulness, in other words.

6 Lundbom, *Jeremiah 21–36*, 352.

7 Ryken, *Jeremiah and Lamentations*, 415.

8 Religious officials in Babylon included "Diviners," who sought "to know and to interpret the will of the gods"; "Chanters," who were employed "to bring the believer into peace with god, if that was necessary, and there to keep him"; 281 and "Astrologers," who committed themselves to the observance and interpretation "of lunar,

solar and stellar phenomena." For the first two classes, see Georges Contenau, *Everyday Life in Babylon and Assyria*, 281; for the third, see D. J. Wiseman, *Nebuchadrezzar and Babylon: The Schweich Lectures* (London: The British Academy, 1991), 88.

9 J. A. Thompson, *The Book of Jeremiah*, The New International Commentary on the Old Testament (Grand Rapids: Eerdmans, 1980), 546.

Chapter 6

1 Richard Dawkins, *The God Delusion* (Boston: Houghton Mifflin, 2006), 31.

2 Christopher Hitchens, *God Is Not Great: How Religion Poisons Everything* (New York: Twelve, 2007), 64.

3 Justin Brierley, *The Surprising Rebirth of Belief in God: Why New Atheism Grew Old and Secular Thinkers Are Considering Christianity Again* (Carol Stream: Tyndale Elevate, 2023), 3.

4 Ayaan Hirsi Ali, "Why I Am Now a Christian: Atheism Can't Equip Us for Civilisational War," UnHerd, November 11, 2023, https://unherd.com/2023/11/why-i-am-now-a-christian.

5 Niall Ferguson, remarks in "Niall Ferguson: Does the West Have a Future?," Macdonald-Laurier Institute, December 22, 2025, https://www.youtube.com/watch?v=XgLglcyZqkY.

6 Ed Boice, "Forrest Frank Surpasses Drake in YouTube Music Listeners," *Rapzilla*, August 18, 2025, https://rapzilla.com/2025-08-forrest-frank-surpasses-drake-youtube-music-listeners.

7 "Christian Charts Trend," Accio, August 25, 2025, https://www.accio.com/business/christian-charts-trend.

8 Emma Madden, "Christian Music Is Experiencing a Pop Breakthrough," NPR, June 13, 2025, https://www.npr.org/2025/06/13/nx-s1-5430545/christian-music-forrest-frank-brandon-lake-popularity?spm=a2700.accio_bizSeo.0.0.1bf57453wrRg4u.

9 Jeffrey A. Trachtenberg, "Bible Sales Surged Following Killing of Charlie Kirk," *Wall Street Journal*, October 20, 2025, https://www.wsj.com/business/media/bible-sales-surged-following-killing-of-charlie-kirk-7da17aec.

10 Mark Duell, "Bible Sales in Britain Hit Record High as Experts Say Interest in Religion Among Gen Z Has Driven a 134% Increase over Past Six Years," *Daily Mail*, January 9, 2026, https://www.dailymail.co.uk/news/article-15449037/Bible-sales-Britain-record-high-Gen-Z-Christian.html.

11 James Marriott, "Full-Fat Faith: The Young Christian Converts Filling Our Churches," *The Times of London*, August 15, 2025, https://www.thetimes.com/comment/columnists/article/full-fat-faith-the-young-christian-converts-filling-our-churches-x69pd289k. For the "quadrupling" data, see Erica Pandey, "Young Men Are Leading a Religious Resurgence," Axios, May 10, 2025, https://www.axios.com/2025/05/10/religious-young-people-christianity-rise.

12 Kaya Burgess, "Gen Z Half as Likely as Their Parents to Identify as Atheists," *The Times of London*, January 25, 2025, https://www.thetimes.com/uk/religion/article/gen-z-half-as-likely-as-their-parents-to-identify-as-atheists-wp2vlol29.

13 "New Barna Data: Young Adults Lead a Resurgence in Church Attendance," Barna Group, September 2, 2025, https://www.barna.com/research/young-adults-lead-resurgence-in-church-attendance.

14 J. I. Packer, *Knowing God* (Wheaton: Crossway, 2023 [1973]), 128–29.

15 Credit to Lundbom for this fruitful biblical connection: *Jeremiah 21–35*, 352.

16 Stephen Foster, "I'm a Barrister—not a Barista," Streams Studio, December 14, 2023, https://www.youtube.com/watch?v=pECvf2lxHOI.

17 Leading Britain's Conversation (X), March 31, 2024, https://x.com/LBC/status/1774510715975368778.

18 Ibid.

Chapter 7

1 American Psychological Association, "Stress in America 2024," October 2024, https://www.apa.org/pubs/reports/stress-in-america/2024.

2 Richard Hofstadter, "The Paranoid Style in American Politics," *Harper's*, November 1964, https://harpers.org/archive/1964/11/the-paranoid-style-in-american-politics.

3 Ibid.

4 See Douglas Wilson, *Mere Christendom* (Moscow, Idaho: Canon Press, 2023); Joseph Boot, *Ruler of Kings: Toward a Christian Vision of Government* (London: Wilberforce Publications, 2022); Greg L. Bahnsen, *Theonomy in Christian Ethics*, 3rd ed. (Nacogdoches: Covenant Media Press, 2002); Stephen Wolfe, *The Case for Christian Nationalism* (Moscow, Idaho: Canon Press, 2022); Andrew Torba and Andrew Isker, *A Biblical Guide to Taking Dominion & Discipling Nations* (No publishing location given; Gab AI, 2022).

5 As I have noted, part of what has made "Christian Nationalism" a challenge for the church is that it comes in numerous iterations. The above ideals, however, do represent a synthesis of nationalist conviction today, and we cannot fail to identify—and respond to—such a synthesis. A movement that hides behind the smokescreen of amorphousness needs engagement all the more.

6 Kidner, *The Message of Jeremiah*, 17.

7 Ibid, 17.

8 Andrew G. Shead, *A Mouth Full of Fire: The Word of God in the Words of Jeremiah*, New Studies in Biblical Theology 29 (Downers Grove: InterVarsity, 2012), 229.

9 Ibid, 229.

10 For more on the atonement, see Steve Jeffery, Michael Ovey, and Andrew Sach, *Pierced for Our Transgressions: Rediscovering the Glory of Penal Substitution* (Wheaton: Crossway, 2007); John Stott, *The Cross of Christ* (Downers Grove: InterVarsity, 1986); Charles Evan Hill and Roger R. Nicole, eds., *The Glory of the Atonement: Biblical, Theological & Practical Perspectives* (Downers Grove: IVP Academic, 2004); J. I. Packer and Mark Dever, *In My Place Condemned He Stood: Celebrating the Glory of the Atonement* (Wheaton: Crossway, 2008); John Owen, *The Death of Death in the*

Death of Christ, repr. ed. (Edinburgh: Banner of Truth Trust, 1999); Owen Strachan, *The Warrior Savior: A Theology of the Work of Christ* (Phillipsburg: P&R, 2024).

11 Garrett, *Understanding Jeremiah*, 223.

12 See Abraham Kuyper, *Lectures in Calvinism* (Grand Rapids: Eerdmans, 2000 [1898]). Other helpful resources on church and state matters include Kevin DeYoung and Greg Gilbert, *What Is the Mission of the Church? Making Sense of Social Justice, Shalom, and the Great Commission* (Wheaton: Crossway, 2011); Jason G. Duesing, Thomas White, and Malcolm B. Yarnell III, *First Freedom: The Beginning and End of Religious Liberty* (Nashville: B&H Academic, 2016); Jeff Moore, "The Mission of the Church and the Mission of the State: Honoring Christ's Authority to Define Proper Domains," *Gloria Deo Journal of Theology* 3 (2024), at https://drive.google.com/file/d/18X3Dv6ni8JecgLt7GVuwommJWUAs-icm/view.

Conclusion

1 Makoto Fujimura, "Kintsugi Grace: Prismatic Art beyond the Rainbow" (2023 Kuyper Prize Acceptance Speech), May 11, 2023, https://makotofujimura.com/writings/kintsugi-grace-prismatic-art-beyond-the-rainbow.

2 Ibid.

3 Peterson, *God of the Garden*, 52.